# Liberation by Encounter a New Perspective on Pure land Buddhism

Cover image by Deming Gao
Translator: Dan Li（李眈）
Editor: Dan Li（李眈）& Jun Wang（王君）

ISBN: 978-1-957144-95-5

Library of Congress Control Number: 2024909043

Published and distributed in May 2024 in the United States

Asian Culture Press LLC
1942 Broadway St., Suite 314c,
Boulder, CO 80302,
United States

For information on reprints, adaptations, or other licensing inquiries, please contact the Author at 1512272986@qq.com

# Introduction

Since Master Shandao propagated the Pure land teachings in the *Three Pure land Sutras* as the method of attaining rebirth in the Pure land, repeating the name of Buddha has become one of the mainstream practices in East Asian Buddhism. Today, from the perspective of lay practitioners in mainland China, Pure land cultivation is considered the absolute mainstream of Buddhist practice. However, perhaps due to the importance of meditation in the monastic practice of Buddhism or the elevated status of Zen Buddhism in Chinese Buddhist tradition, the understanding of the conditions for rebirth in the Pure land is somewhat associated with the requirement of "single-mindedness without being distracted" in repeating. This "single-mindedness", often understood as a meditative state achieved through repeating of Amitābha, is not easy to be attained through regular but intermittent repeating by lay practitioners. Similarly, "auspicious signs at the time of death" are often cited as one of the indications of rebirth. Over time, these ideas have solidified within the Chinese Pure land tradition and have become long-standing beliefs for many Pure land practitioners, although their basis in Buddhist scriptures is never definitive. The standard of rebirth attainment becoming unattainable, the lay practitioners experience anguish and anxiety about their liberation at the end of this life. The Cundi Buddhist College aims to address the dilemma faced by lay practitioners torn between worldly responsibilities fulfillment and transcendent liberation seek. How can this dilemma be resolved?

On the other hand, Chinese Buddhist history had witnessed a period of prosperity followed by a decline and loss of many Buddhist scriptures during the reign of Emperor Wuzong in Tang Dynasty. Starting from Song Dynasty, Buddhist practice trends in China can be characterized as the convergence of Zen and Pure land practices. Master Taixu more accurately referred to the practice since the late Song Dynasty as "formal schools of Buddhism Tai, Chan, Xian, all converge to Pure land practice." This approach combines the Zen school's meditation practice with the Pure land practice, i.e., repeating employed as a means to achieve the state of Zen awakening. Master Yinguang later achieved significant progress in "surpassing Zen and surpassing the Vinaya" through his teachings, emphasizing the practice of Pure land Buddhism by lay practitioners through "diligent cultivation of pure (land) karma." In contemporary times, "diligent cultivation of pure karma" remains the guiding principle for Chinese Pure land believers. However, the dilemma still remained unresolved for the lay practitioners in their practices. Does the practice of continuous repeating throughout one's life, relying on it as the ultimate means, imply that a lay practitioner must constantly devote all their time to repeating? Is continuity of consciousness of repeating Amitābha in a strict sense, possible for a lay person, even during sleep? When can a lay practitioner be certain of their future rebirth? Additionally, Master Taixu also criticized Master Yinguang for only prescribing Confucian ethics and virtues to Pure land practitioners, arguing that it overlooks other worldly values ignored by Confucianism, such as "scientific, philosophical, literary, artistic, and academic pursuits." In sum, the traditional Pure land School's response to the dilemma faced by contemporary lay practitioners' practice remains ambiguous.

From a practical perspective, as the founder of the Cundi Buddhist College, I have encountered Pure land believers who initially struggled with the concept of liberation in Pure land. They held the belief that the more they recited the Buddha's name, the deeper their practice became, and the fewer distractions they experienced during recitation, the greater their chances of rebirth in the Pure land. This idea naturally led to anxiety about attaining liberation at the time of death and a contradiction between their worldly accomplishments and spiritual liberation. How can an ordinary person with responsibilities for worldly achievements, work, maintaining relationships, and family care allocate all their time and energy to reciting the Buddha's name in a state close to Samadhi without conflicting with the demands of important worldly pursuits?

We, the Cundi Buddhist College, basing on the unique classic for Cundi Buddhist school, *The Exoteric and Esoteric Essentials for Buddhahood Attainment*, outlines the ways for lay Buddhists to joyfully fulfill their worldly values. Blessed by Cundi Bodhisattva, the practitioners enhance their achievements and wisdom, improving the family relationship and making progress in their career. In other words, they rely on the power of the Buddha to create value and benefit for themselves and society. From the experiences of Yuan Liaofan, a lay practitioner in Ming Dynasty, to recent reports of the increased well-being of Cundi practitioners, it is evident that the Cundi Dharma significantly enhances the blessings and well-being of lay practitioners. At the same time, "The Essential Collection" also presents a hidden path of transcendence, namely, the harmonization of Cundi Dharma with the Pure land tradition, as expressed in the final return to Amitabha's Pure land in the Mahayana tradition's Universal Bodhisattva's Aspiration chapter of *Flower Adornment Sutra*. The Cundi Bodhisattva was originally a manifestation of Avalokiteshvara Bodhisattva. The Cundi Dharma's ultimate convergence with all other Dharma ways, flow into Amitabha's Pure land, as is fitting for their practitioners.

In other words, the Cundi Dharma provides lay practitioners with a global solution of practicing Buddhism in the human realm between life and death. The fundamental issue faced by Buddhist believers, the "Life and Death" issue, must be entrusted to the vow power of Amitabha Buddha. This brings us back to the initial question of Pure land Buddhism: what standards must be satisfied to be reborn in the Western Pure land of Ultimate Bliss?

The Buddha Shakyamuni, with his great wisdom and compassion, foreseeing the problem of sentient beings more than two thousand years later, not only answers these questions but also offers detailed explanations. The standards for rebirth in the Pure land are found in the section on the *Nine Grades of Rebirth* of *The Sutra On The Contemplation Of The Buddha Of Infinite Life Delivered By Śākyamuni Buddha* (We call it *Contemplation Sutra* in this work). Those in the lower grade of rebirth simply need to encounter good spiritual advisors at the time of death, receive instructions to entrust themselves to Amitayus Buddha, and recite the name of Amitabha Buddha ten times, "NaMo Amitabha." They will then attain rebirth in the Land of Ultimate Bliss. What does it mean to recite the Buddha's name and what constitutes the end of life? The answers may vary greatly. We will also supply explanations and views to these issues. The Nine Grades of Rebirth may seem like a list of rebirth levels, but in essence, they represent the core standards for rebirth in the Pure land.

Master Shandao extensively clarifies this point in his commentary on the sutra. We will provide an interpretation of the Nine Grades of Rebirth in line with the Three Sutras and Master Shandao's teachings on *Contemplation Sutra*. Although seemingly the Nine Grades of Rebirth are unrelated with one another, there is a fundamental principle that categorizes them, and the clearest explanation can be found in Master Shandao's *Commentary on the Contemplation Sutra*, which was lost in China for a thousand years. Master Shandao summarizes the concept of liberation through encountering favorable conditions, which goes beyond the scope of the Pure land Dharma Approach. It is in line with the Buddhist principle of dependent origination and emptiness, and it serves as a guideline for selecting Buddhist Dharma Approaches that are consistent with Mahayana humanistic Buddhism. We will elaborate on this concept in detail in this document.

Although our interpretations may differ from those of traditional Pure land, we do not claim that our interpretation of Pure land liberation, based on the scriptures, is universally correct or the solely correct version. Our understanding of the conditions for rebirth in the Pure land and our attitude towards alternative interpretations of these conditions are based on a significant insight found in Master Shandao's *Commentary on the Contemplation Sutra*:

In Volume 4 of the *Commentary on the Contemplation Sutra*, a passage that has long been overlooked discusses the concept of liberation through encountering favorable conditions:

*Question: "If practitioners, different from ordinary people in practices and behaviors, encounter various hindrances and disturbances created by evil and deluded individuals, or encounter doubts and difficulties, may not attain rebirth. Or someone might say, 'All of you sentient beings, throughout countless kalpas in the past and in this life, have committed the ten evil deeds, the five heinous acts, the four heavy offenses; slandered the Dharma, the Supreme Beings; broken precepts; and held wrong views in relation to all ordinary and noble beings. These offenses, if not completely eradicated, will inevitably lead to the realms of the three evil paths. How is it possible that by cultivating merit and mindfulness of the Buddha in this life, one can be reborn in the Pure land of no outflows and no birth, attaining enlightenment forever without retrogression?'"*

*Answer: "The Buddha' practices and teachings, as numerous as the grains of sand in the Ganges River, cater for different conditions and mental capacities. They are similar to things in the world that can be seen and believed by human eyes, such as light dispelling darkness, space accommodating things, the earth supporting and nurturing beings, and water giving rise to and moistening life. Fire can bring about both creation and destruction. These are all referred to as relative phenomena, and they are visible to the eye in their countless ways of differences. How much more so for the inconceivable power of the Dharma of the Buddhas, which surely has various benefits. When a particular relative dharma is abandoned, you are leaving a realm of afflictions. When one accepts a particular teaching, one enters a door of liberation and wisdom. Therefore, practitioners, following conditions and engaging in practices, seek liberation in various ways. Why do you obstruct yourself by claiming that the practice with conditions only favorable to your particular case is essential to all sentient beings? What I cherish is the practice favorable to my particular conditions, which is not what you seek; What you cherish is the practice favorable to your particular conditions, which is not what I seek. Hence, practitioners should engage in the practices they*

*delight in, through which they will swiftly attain liberation.*
*Practitioners should understand that if they want to take*
*the path to liberation without obstruction, from ordinary*
*beings to noble beings or even Buddhas, they should take*
*to learning. They should rely on teachings with conditions*
*favorable to themselves, in order that they gain maximal*
*output out of minimal input.*" (CBETA, T37, no. 1753, p.
272, b23-c15.)

Buddhist practitioners encounter various good spiritual
advisors, situations, and opportune circumstances. The
methods and interpretations of the teachings they embrace
also vary. We practice according to different individual
conditions and find joy in practice suitable for us; people
attain their liberation through the ways appropriate to them.
Therefore, we refer to the Pure land Approach based on
Master Shandao's teachings as the Theory of liberation
through encountering favorable conditions in Mahayana
Buddhism.

# CONTENTS

Chapter

# 1

## The Establishment of the Pure land Dharma Way and the Concept of Liberation by Encounter

# 1.1 Lay Practitioners and the Mahayana Path of Pure land Attainment

In the Dharma-ending Age, whether Buddhist practice can be engaged for a secular being depends on the establishment of the Pure land Dharma Approach, without which one must become a monastic in order to practice Buddhism. Only when the Pure land Dharma Way is established can practitioners can engage in transcendent practice in this secular world. Without the horizontal access leading beyond the three realms, the only solution is the vertical path, relying on self-power and gradual progressing through the levels of the three realms to eradicate afflictions. This is the path of monastic practice. The distinction between the easy access and the difficult access in Mahayana Buddhist practice was first mentioned in Nagarjuna Bodhisattva's *Ten Stages Treatise* (Daśabhūmika-vibhāṣā ), which states,

"The Buddha Dharma has immeasurable approaches, just as worldly paths have easy and difficult ones. To attain an aim, walking on land is more difficult than riding a boat on water. Such is the case with The path of a Bodhisattva. Some diligently engage in practice and progress swiftly through expedient means based on faith." It also says, "Pay homage to Buddhas and reverently repeat the names of Amitabha Buddha and other Buddhas." "If a person recites my name and aspires to be reborn in my land, that person will definitely attain the ultimate enlightenment of Anuttara-samyak-sambodhi." The difficult access refers to a practice that emphasizes diligent and continuous self-cultivation, while the easy path is based on faith of other-power. Therefore, Pure land, as an easy access, is a suitable Dharma Approach for lay practitioners.

Seemingly regarded as one of the sects within Mahayana Buddhism, The Pure land Dharma Approach is parallel to other Mahayana Dharma paths. However, in Land of Ultimate Bliss—it is the differentiating factor between Mahayana Buddhism and Hinayana Buddhism. In a strict sense, Hinayana Buddhism accepts neither the existence of Amitabha Buddha's Pure land of Ultimate Bliss, nor the idea that we can be reborn in the Pure land of Ultimate Bliss at the end of this life. The existence of the Pure land of Ultimate Bliss is furthest from the worldview of Hinayana Buddhism because, in the strictest sense, adherents of Hinayana faith cannot comprehend the wisdom and merits of the attainment of Buddhahood. On the other hand, the Pure land Dharma Way, ranging from the realm of Buddhahood to sentient beings, is purely established by the merits of Buddhahood, Both Mahayana and Hinayana Buddhism aim to liberate individuals from the suffering of samsara and the afflictions of birth and death. In Hinayana Buddhism, individuals liberate through their own efforts, while in Mahayana Buddhism, liberating others from afflictions is essential to one's own liberation. Therefore, the attainments obtained by each are different. Hinayana practitioners can attain Arhatship, while Mahayana practitioners can attain Buddhahood. The fruit of Arhathood in Hinayana Buddhism cannot directly contribute to the liberation of others, while the fruit of Buddhahood in Mahayana Buddhism includes the realization of the Pure land as the fulfillment of the Buddha's vow and directly involves the liberation of other sentient beings. With extremely low thresholds, The Pure land of Ultimate Bliss, embracing the sentient beings and endowing them with Fruit of Buddhahood, perfectly manifests the unfathomable merits of Buddhahood in its inseparable aspects of self-benefit and others-benefits, which cannot be accommodated in Hinayana Buddhism viewpoint. In practice, the existence of the Pure land of Ultimate Bliss and the establishment of the Pure land Dharma Approach determines the legitimacy of engaged secular practice as well as liberation attainment. Otherwise, we can but embark on the arduous and lengthy journey of self-liberation in this impure world, following the path of renunciation of secular world in Hinayana Buddhism. Therefore, by encouraging more people to engage in secular life and simultaneously have faith in the Pure land Dharma Approach, one can take the path of a Bodhisattva, practicing self-cultivation while saving others along the way.

## 1.2 Fruit of Buddhahood and individual capacities.

Similarly, our understanding of the Pure land as the fruition of Buddhism extends to our attitude towards the "capacity" of practitioners in Mahayana Buddhism. Buddhist practitioners often regard Buddha mindfulness & Pure land cultivators inferior to Zen & Esoteric Buddhism practitioners. Pure land practitioners themselves with this view often feel somewhat abased. However, when practitioners consider the concept of capacity from the angle of the Buddhahood fruition, a different perspective emerges. Buddhism, as a teaching of the Dharma, is itself the fruition of diligent efforts of those with great superior capacities, just as one reaps the fruits of farming through hard work. So, who enjoys these fruits? It is the practitioners with average or inferior capacities after this fulfilled Buddha.

In reality, those with superior capacities serve and aide the practitioners with average or inferior capacities. As practitioners with inferior capacities, we should be grateful to those with superior capacities for their qualities, practice, and merits, for fruits of Buddhahood bestowed upon us. The saintly monastics embody this virtue. The supreme individual is evidently the Bodhisattva Dharmakara, who later became Amitabha Buddha, and compared to him, all practitioners in the Dharma-ending age are individuals with inferior capacities.

On the other hand, in the conventional understanding there is a misconception that capacity in Buddhism is equated with natural gift. It is believed that individuals with different natural qualities or merits possess superior capacities are able to quickly and correctly understand the teachings of Buddhism and progress in practices such as meditation, while those with average or inferior capacities are seen as the opposite. Accordingly, the distinction between individuals with superior and inferior capacities is considered clear, and one can easily discern their own capacity, while the good spiritual advisors or teachers can more easily discern the distinctive capacities of their disciples. However, in the *Sutra of Perfect Enlightenment*, there is another understanding of capacity: "Good sons, all sentient beings possess perfect enlightenment. In their encounter with good spiritual advisors, they rely on the practices and stages according to those advisors' teachings. Their enlightenment can be sudden or gradual. If they encounter the Tathagata's supreme bodhi and the right path of practice, there is no distinction in the size or level of their capacity—they all attain the fruition of Buddhahood. If various sentient beings seek good spiritual friends but encounter those with wrong views, they fail to attain proper awakening. This is called the seed-nature of evil teachers, who deviate the multitude but the consequence is not to be attributed to the fault of sentient beings. It is called the differentiation of the five natures of sentient beings." It can be seen that capacity is not determined by people's personal endowments but by their encounter with good spiritual advisors and the latter's teachings. From the perspective of attainment of Buddhahood, there is no difference in capacity among practitioners who encounter a great spiritual advisor and enter the right path of practice, as "there is no distinction in the size or level of their capacity—they all attain Buddhahood." Simply put, the intention of the *Sutra of Perfect Enlightenment* is: *the capacity is determined by the teacher*. In reality, we cannot judge by ourselves our own capacities. When we encounter a spiritual advisor who teaches the Dharma Way appropriate to our individual circumstances, practicing accordingly is considered in accordance with our sharp or superior capacity, which flows from our encounter with the advisor. The assertion in the Sutra regarding the evaluation of sentient beings' capacities from the perspective of the Buddha's fruition aligns with the concept of liberation by encountering favorable conditions. Now let us return to the Pure land Dharma Approach. The establishment of the Pure land Dharma Approach originates from the fruition of the Buddha's virtues, and our acceptance of the Pure land Dharma Approach is also rooted in our understanding of the causal relationship in Buddhism.

# 1.3 Deduction of Liberation through encounter of favorable conditions

Now let's briefly deduce the proposition of liberation through hetu-pratyaya (factors of dependent origination) encounter in light of causality. People's encounter with and faith in the Pure land Dharma are not solely due to their current cultivation but also the effect of their past-life practices. Similarly, encounter with the Pure land Dharma in this present life and rebirth attainment in the Pure land after this life are the accumulated result of countless past-life practices and the summarized achievements of this life's cultivation. The Pure land, as the fruition vehicle, operates on its initiator and its receivers in a similar way with respect to time. The existence of the Pure land is the result of the aeons of cultivation by the monk Dharmakara, who eventually became Amitabha Buddha; Individuals' reception of Amitabha's original vow and rebirth in the Pure land also result from their past-life practices.

In past countless lives, we have accumulated abundant merits and virtues, which enable us to encounter the Pure land Dharma Approach in this life and have the karmic affinities for understanding and believing in it. The Buddha's statement that "those with few virtuous roots, blessings, karmic affinities are less likely to be reborn in the Pure land of the Buddha" encompasses the accumulated merits of past lives. In view of Buddhist dependent origination theory, causes and conditions are both regarded as necessary factors and interdependent determinations, with primary conditions named causes and secondary conditions as interdependent determinations. Different conditions combined give rise to different outcomes.

In human life, a person's body, speech, mind, behavior, combined with the environmental conditions at the time constitute causes, they further develop into the latent karmic power, and finally produce future karmic results. The actual manifestation of these consequences depends on the appropriate convergence of conditions. As life continues, the fruition combined with various conditions encountered presently, is taken as another cause and further gives rise to future results. Therefore, the most important factor in both the categories of causes and conditions within the Buddhist discourse is the encounter or receiveing of various conditions and causes.

How do we define the karmic force that drives the manifestation of karmic consequences in one's life, as well as the conditions when the consequences appear? A certain species of seed will grow into a particular type of tree, but it requires sunlight, air, water, and soil in the right time and place for the tree to manifest. The seed not only contains the blueprint of the future tree but also outlines the external conditions required for it to become a tree. The appropriate conditions are pre-determined within the causes, and they are completed when the consequences manifest.

For the Pure land Dharma, "liberation through encounter"means that the fruition of the merits and virtues from your past-life practice has matured, and in this lifetime, you encounter the corresponding karmic conditions that correspond to the merits you have cultivated. These encounters include encounter with certain people and receiving certain Dharma. They determine the kind of Dharma approach you adopt and the way you interpret and understand the Pure land. After all, people, known as good spiritual advisors in Buddhism, transmit Dharma ways, and different spiritual advisors have different interpretations of the Dharma. The magnitude and types of merits accumulated in past lives determine whom we encounter as teachers and what kind of Dharma approach we encounter in this life.

Believing in the Dharma way taught by a good spiritual advisor and practicing accordingly is considered an effective encounter. The encounter with the teacher and the Dharma the teacher imparts determine the form of one's Pure land faith. The Pure land Dharma Approach is approached through faith, and different encounters give rise to different forms of faith. The forms of faith in the Pure land practiced by Buddhists consist of two elements: the object of faith and the degree of faith. The object of faith differs from person to person: some believe that reciting Mahayana scriptures alone can lead to rebirth in the Pure land; some believe that reciting the Buddha's name alone can lead to rebirth; some believe that reciting the Buddha's name at the time of death is necessary for rebirth; some believe that rebirth requires unwavering single-mindedness in recitation of name of Buddha; some believe that to achieve rebirth, one must repeat Buddha name seven days and nights to maintain single-mindedness; some believe that all karmic forces must be purified for rebirth to occur. Different objects of faith lead to different degrees of faith, including unwavering faith, half-belief, or varying degrees of conviction. The forms of faith in the Pure land are determined by the type of Dharma way and the kind of teachers that we encounter. The teachers that we encounter through hetu-pratyaya (factors of dependent origination) appear to us with affinities. We have faith in and adhere to the Dharma way they teach. Different affinities and encounters actually reflect the differences in past-life cultivation. Thus, an individual's past-life cultivation determines their affinities through encounter, and the differences in people's cultivation history determine the differences in their encountered affinities. The differences in the affinities encountered, whether we like the teacher and the dharma way they pronounce, determine the various forms of faith for each individual, and within the forms of faith, the conditions for rebirth are prescribed. Based on the prescribed conditions for rebirth within the respective forms of faith, one follows them, and if accomplished, rebirth occurs; if not accomplished, one enters the Pure land region of Suspicion where one is unable to receive Buddha due to one's doubts about the Three Jewels of Buddha, Faith and Sangha.

Past life cultivation, karmic affinities encounter, faith in the Pure land, rebirth in the Pure land based on faith in conditions for rebirth and the corresponding present-life practice thereafter— all these constitute a series of cause-and-effect relationships.

In the history of Pure land Buddhism, faith has often been emphasized as the sole means of entry into the Pure land, while the differences in faith have not been highlighted. It is important to understand that people are fully justified for their choice of faith, which derives from their past-life karma. Different faiths lead to different practices, but as long as they cherish the same aspiration for rebirth in the Pure land, they can be born there. Reciting Mahayana scriptures can lead to rebirth in the Pure land, so can single-mindedly reciting the Buddha's name or reciting it ten times on deathbed. Different faiths are not contradictory when viewed separately, because individuals have their own beliefs. Just as birth and death fall upon each individual person and cannot be shared, each person's faith is suited to themselves. We should not insist that our personal understanding of the Pure land is universally right for everyone. When we proclaim our understanding of the Pure land, if the listeners accept and appreciate it, they practice accordingly and attain liberation. If they don't, they leave immediately without further ado, which is determined by their past-life karma and present situation. We will not say that the latter's understanding of the conditions for rebirth in the Pure land is incorrect or contradicts the sutras. Their past-life cultivation determines how one sutra enters each person's heart and manifests in various forms. They may not like my expounding of the sutras due to the differences in our respective affinities, temperaments, personalities, etc.. In short, an individuals' beliefs and practices are largely determined by their past-life causes and deeds. In the endless river of reincarnation, each life's direction has already been determined, to a great extent, by the karma of their past-life. Encounter with the Pure land Dharma Approach is already a great blessing, which won't happen without virtuous roots, as our Buddha says. The differences in individual faiths represent the differences in the inclination of individual lives, and each has its own individual karmic basis and reasons.

Buddhist practitioners' belief system based on their particular situation, is the result of their past-life karmic forces, in conjunction with the people and the Dharma they encounter in this life. There is no contradiction between two individuals' different faiths. People's joy in and devotion to a belief manifest their past-life karma and accumulated merit. Those with abundant merits firmly believe in the existence of the Pure land, in the power of Amitabha Buddha, and are confident that Amitabha will guide them upon their departure from this land. Others, with different merits, have other objects of faith. They believe that they must recite the Buddha's name continuously for seven days and nights without distraction in order to attract Amitabha Buddha's guidance to the Pure land. The differences in past-life cultivation and karmic affinities lead to differences in the paths of liberation. Ultimately, the differences in faith reflect the variations in individual inclinations and are caused by the differences in their individual karma.

In the past, people have separated "faith" from the causal perspective in the fundamental framework of Buddhist thinking. Different forms of faith were not attributed to the differences in personal past karma but were seen as inherent variations in consciousness. They are seen as different interpretations of the sutra, which more or less deviate from the only one right interpretation, so the different interpretations are considered irreconcilable logical contradictions and conceptual conflicts. Some have claimed that ten recitations of the Buddha's name are sufficient for rebirth, while others insist that single-mindedness is a necessity. These perspectives result in mutual accusations of promoting false teachings. For example, Chinese Pure land Buddhism has long rejected Japanese Jodo Shinshu as a "deviant sect" for the latter's emphasis on faith as the primary cause and reliance on reciting the Buddha's name, while Jodo Shinshu also views traditional Chinese Pure land Buddhism, which advocates single-minded recitation of the Buddha's name, as going against Amitabha Buddha's original vow. It is dangerous to attack one another for their different forms of faith. The 18th vow of Amitabha Buddha states, "If, when I attain buddhahood, sentient beings in the lands of the ten directions who sincerely and joyfully entrust themselves to me, desire to be born in my land, and think of me even ten times should not be born there, may I not attain perfect enlightenment. Excluded, however, are those who commit the five heinous offenses and *abuse the Right Dharma.* "In the *Contemplation Sutra*, the inferior class of rebirth includes those who commit the Five heinous Offenses and the Ten Evil Deeds, but *slanderer of the correct Dharma is excluded from salvation.* Therefore, we should refrain from defaming different beliefs regarding rebirth, and we should not defame any Buddhist Dharma way as illegitimate. This is not to say that we don't have our own understanding of the Buddha's teachings that we hold firmly. We maintain our own standpoint and beliefs to be only suitable for us. According to *Contemplation Sutra*, even the Five heinous Offenders and the Ten Evil Doers, will be accepted into the lowest grade but slanderers of the right Dharma are denied the access to the Pure land. Therefore, we should not slander or defame different beliefs about rebirth, nor should we defame any Buddhist Dharma way as illegitimate. The Pure land, as the manifestation of the Buddha's merits, is inconceivable for human reason, and the paths leading to it are not singular. If we consider one path as true and regard all others as false, we are viewing the Buddha's fruition from the perspective of cyclic secular existence, thereby generating secular cyclic views.

Each Buddhist practitioner has their particular form of faith, which is subordinate to their Dharma Way and determined by the karmic conditions and spiritual affinities they encounter. Their joy and dedication in upholding their faith are manifestations of their past karmic causes and accumulated merits. Those with great merits firmly believe in the existence of the Pure land upon hearing about it. They have faith in the power of Amitabha Buddha and believe that He will guide them upon their death. On the other hand, some practitioners have different karmic conditions. They set the requirement for themselves to continuously recite the Buddha's name for seven days and nights without distractions in the hope that Amitabha Buddha will receive them to the Pure land. These differences in past karmic causes and spiritual affinities result in diverse paths to liberation. Ultimately, these differences arise from variations in karmic affinities and blessings.

Each person's faith contains essentially a norm they set for themselves, by which they evaluate their practice. It is unrelated to the faith of others or the standards others establish. We cannot take a universal and overarching stand, claiming that the practitioners who attain unwavering mindfulness have a higher level of cultivation than those who simply have strong faith in the Pure land, or the former have higher probability of rebirth in Pure land. Nor can we say that the practitioners who fail to attain single-mindedness in repeating Buddha name have a lower probability of rebirth in the Pure land due to their distracted state of mind. As ordinary sentient beings, we cannot penetrate into others' minds or foresee their future outcomes, nor can we discern their practices, actions, and karmic consequences from past lives. Therefore, we are unable to compare the forms of faith held by different individuals against a specific objective criterion.

Any of our attempts to dissuade practitioners of different forms of Pure land faith from their practice by saying their perspectives are incorrect or incompatible with the scriptures, is likely to provoke criticism. As ordinary human beings, we are denied of the Buddha insights into the unbeginning karmic actions underlying different viewpoints. We should not pull ourselves up to the omniscience possessed only by Buddha and judge the goodness or probability of rebirth for each individual.

This does not mean that we lack our own understanding of Buddhist principles. Each of us maintains our own standpoint and faith. However, our faith only holds validity for us and those sharing the standpoint. We shall never defame the paths of other practitioners, our siblings on different paths leading to the same destination.

Ultimately, blessings, encounters and karmic affinities determine the diverse forms of faith in the Pure land. Chinese Buddhists translate interdependent origination, at concrete level, as *YuanFen*, meaning condition-destiny. It means that people's conditions lead to their destiny. Blessings manifest as karmic affinities. Karmic affinities arise from encounters, but the distributed destiny returns to each individual. The belief in the Pure land ultimately belongs to oneself and concerns one's own journey.

Now, why do different individuals hold different perspectives despite the fact that rebirth is the same goal to all and the three Pure land sutras exist as scriptures on the same Pure land, such that they can be said to be the same sutra? We emphasize that the individualization of faith arises through the encounter and karmic affinities with particular spiritual advisers and Dharma interpretations. Therefore, such a principle accommodates various forms of faith, including different perspectives or standpoints. Does this accommodation conflict with the objective nature of rebirth and the scriptures? However, the truths presented in the scriptures also require transmission through faith and interpretation as an intermediary when they are in our hand, comprehended by us. Faith itself is intertwined with all that happened in the unbeginning cycles of individual lives. The interpretation of the scriptures and the interpretation that one adheres to are ultimately matters of individual blessings and karmic affinities. In countless rivers there are reflections of countless moons, which do not conflict with one another because of the distinct nature of each river. Why do we perceive a conflict between the objective universality of rebirth in the Pure land theory and the subjective diversity of individual faith? Humans tend to mistake the reflection of the moon for the moon itself, therefore taking their own faith as the universal and correct truth,

The Pure land tradition emphasizes faith-based entry

into the Pure land. The reason-based entry, however, is very likely to evoke defamation of Dharma, namely the standards for rebirth in the Pure land being either this or that, but the fact is that these standards are inherently diverse and this diversity also becomes individualized through different interpretations and practices of individual in situation. From the perspective of reason-based entry, the question of whether rebirth is achieved through ten repetitions of the Buddha name, a single-minded repeating, or unwavering mindfulness, must be single-choice question. What is the criteria for entry to the Pure land? However, the theoretical exploration involves our own intellectual contemplation of the Buddha wisdom, and the gap between our intellect and Buddha wisdom is evident. If the Pure land Dharma Approach required reason-based entry, then deviations and wavering, as well as constant change of viewpoints, which are inherent to human understandings, would follow. People differ from one another in their practices and intellects. What they understand also varies with their experiences and cultivation. On the other hand, faith is something other than understanding or reason. Faith can remain constant, for example, we consistently believe that the world exists externally and does not change as we wish. If at some point in our lives we begin to trust in the primal vow of Amitabha Buddha and entrust our birth and death to him, we can be free from worries about liberation after death until the end of our lives. In general, faith is more steadfast than reason, as faith relies more on individual blessings and karmic affinities than reason.

# 1.4 The Affinity with Dharma in Love and Joy

The theme of liberation by encounter is not our invention but derives from a question-and-response part of the *Commentary on the Contemplation Sutra* by Master Shandao. Let us briefly analyze this passage by Master Shandao in his *Commentary on the Contemplation Sutra*, Volume 4:

*Question: "If practitioners have practices and behaviors differ from those of ordinary people, encounter various hindrances and disturbances created by evil and deluded individuals, or encounter doubts and difficulties, they may not attain rebirth. Or someone might say, 'All of you sentient beings, throughout countless kalpas in the past and in this present life, have committed ten evil actions, the five rebellious acts, the four heavy offenses, the slandering of the Dharma, or the Supreme Beings, the breaking of precepts, and the holding of wrong views in relation to all ordinary and noble beings. These offenses have not been completely eradicated. These offenses are bound to lead to the realms of the three evil destinies. How is it possible that by cultivating merit and mindfulness of the Buddha in this present life, one can be reborn in the Pure land of no outflows and no birth, attaining enlightenment forever without retrogression?'"*

*Answer: "The practices and teachings of the Buddhas based on different conditions and mental capacities are as numerous as the grains of sand in the Ganges River. Even the relative phenomena in the world, such as light dispelling darkness, space accommodating things, the earth supporting and nurturing, water giving rise to life and moistening, and fire creating or destructing, are visible to human eyes in their countless different ways. Surely the inconceivable power of the Dharma of the Buddhas has various benefits. When a particular relative dharma is abandoned, you are leaving a realm of afflictions. When one accepts a particular teaching, one enters a door of liberation and wisdom. Therefore, practitioners, following conditions and engaging in practices, seek liberation in various ways. Why do you obstruct me by claiming that the practice with conditions only favorable to your particular case is essential to me? What I cherish and love, is the practice that suits me through hetu-pratyaya (factors of dependent origination), which is not what you seek. What you cherish and love is the practice that suits you, that accords with you through hetu-pratyaya (factors of dependent origination), which is not what I seek and does not accord with me. Hence, practitioners should engage in the practice they delight in, and they will swiftly attain liberation. Practitioners should understand that if they want to understand the principles and teachings of liberation, for ordinary beings to noble beings and even the path to the fruition of Buddhahood, they can learn and understand everything without obstruction. But if they want to practice the path, they should rely on Dharmas with conditions favorable to their individual being, so that they will gain maximal benefits out of minimal input."* (CBETA, T37, no. 1753, p. 272, b23-c15.)

In this passage, Master Shandao poses questions from

two types of people who dissuade a practitioner from attaining rebirth. The first type of dissuader is also a Pure land practitioner. According to his view, Master Shandao cannot attain rebirth because his understanding of the Pure land scriptures and the corresponding practice differs from theirs. The second type of skeptic is not a Pure land practitioner but a Buddhist learner who believes that Pure land rebirth based on Buddhist doctrines outside the Pure land Sutras is impossible. Traditionally, Pure land followers tend to emphasize the refutation of the second type of skeptic. However, in our contemporary context, the question is not whether Pure land itself is established relative to other traditions; this issue has been resolved since Pure land became a major denomination of east Asian Buddhism. The issue we face now is the position of the first type of dissuader within the Pure land faith community. They hold different standards for rebirth in the Pure land, and within Pure land believer community, different interpretations and conceptions among different factions are considered as the only correct criterion by which we judge whether others can attain rebirth. Master Shandao refutes both types of dissuaders. Why? Both types share a feature: they insist that their views and practice guidelines are universally applicable to anyone and the only correct ones for everyone. Their attachment to their own point of view, arises not only from their understanding of Buddha's intention, but they wrap it up in a universal cloak. However, the problem is that Buddhist scriptures and Dharma ways are not singular but multiple, and each person's mind is different. As a result from contact with the Dharma, each individual's understanding and manifestation of the teachings and beliefs are different. Therefore, Master Shandao refutes both types of dissuaders and states his own argument in two steps. In the first step, he demonstrates the rich and diverse nature of Buddhist teachings: "As numerous as particles of dust, all Buddhas' teachings are adaptive to sentient beings for their respective capacities and circumstances." Although only Shakyamuni Buddha appeared in the world of Saha, in the Mahayana world, there are countless Buddhas. Each Buddha followed a different path during their cultivation, and after attaining Buddhahood, they taught Dharma ways based on the appropriate circumstances. It can be said that there are as many Dharma ways as there are sentient beings with different aptitudes and circumstances. What happens between a Dharma way and the sentient beings that embrace it is mutual suitability, mutual adaptation, and mutual satisfaction—so-called "Approach of Relativity". The concept of "Relativity" is often conceived to be away from the highest level of spiritual enlightenment in Chinese Mahayana tradition or to be not absolute, which is, however, not stressed here. "The relativity" here does not have any negative connotation but another way of expressing interdependent origination, specifically designating the reciprocity between phenomena, their complementarity with each other, and suitability between concave and convex. "When a particular relative dharma is abandoned, you are leaving a realm of afflictions. When one accepts a particular teaching, one enters a door of liberation and wisdom." When a person enters a Dharma door, they are like complementary concave and convex shapes forming a complete whole. When a person practices a Dharma way, s/he will attain liberation.

The second step of the argument is more crucial and concerns individual practitioners. What accords with my aptitude and conditions is not only a Dharma Approach or an understanding, but rather my practice. In a board sense, all of a practitioner's actions could actually be considered as their practice, or specifically as their Buddhist practice in a narrow sense. However, the fact is that from the moment we have faith in Buddhism, our actions as a whole, every action, are imbued with Buddhist coloration. Regardless of the broad or narrow difference, our "practice" arises from favorable conditions. We adopt a specific Dharma approach in accordance with our aptitudes, and give rise to such individualized versions of practice that matches ourselves and the Dharma Approach. But how should this corresponding practice, based on favorable encounter, manifest and express itself? "What I cherish and love, is the practice that suits me through hetu-pratyaya (factors of dependent origination)." Therefore, both types of individuals dissuade me from attaining rebirth mainly on the following basis: they impose on me what they love while ignoring what they love is only what suits them but may not suit me. *What they love is not what I seek.* Master Shendao is unequivocal. What I cherish is my practice in accordance with conditions favorable to me, and he further explains what I cherish is what brings me joy. "Practitioners should engage in the practice they delight in, and they will swiftly attain liberation." What brings me joy and what I love constitute favorable conditions for me. Therefore, each person should cultivate the practice that brings them joy according to their own situations, and they will surely attain liberation swiftly. Two brothers reach the mountain tops through different paths, yet in harmony with each other. Finally, Master Shandao adds that learning&understanding Buddha's teachings is different from practicing them with love&joy. Practice with love&joy depends entirely on the individualized, favorable conditions, for an individual, in its relation to one particular Dharma way. Following such a Dharma path gives the sign for a speedy attainment. The Dharmas that bring love and joy to particular person are very limited in number and very narrow in scope. On the other hand, understanding relies on rationality, which does not require individualized affinity (joy and love) as a sign of good path, and all principles and virtuous practices are equal from the perspective of understanding. The scope of the objects of understanding is very wide. Our practice is based on the Dharma that brings us love and joy, which is a sign that it is accordance with favorable conditions, or encounters. It is individualized and represents the fastest and most effective path to liberation for ourselves. The manifestation of the Dharma way that accords with one individual is their love and joy for it in its practice. Faith and the attitudinal, individualized approach to one Buddhist teaching and its practice, rather than the universality, abstraction, and concept-based cognition based on rationality in studying and understanding all Buddhist teachings, is the fast track to liberation.

## 1.5   The Diversity and Unity of the Pure land Doctrine

The above is Master Shandao's concept of liberation through affinity. Prior to Master Shandao, no one had clearly proposed such a framework for interpreting the Pure land doctrine, such that all Buddhist denominations can be accommodated with it and the disputes within the Pure land school can be resolved. After Master Shandao, his insightful and harmonious assertions based on dependent origination and emptiness were not given much attention due to the long-term loss of his *Commentary on the Contemplation Sutra in Four Fascicles*. Our assertions are an extension of Master Shandao's insights, based further on the causal relationship that *Amitabha sutra* asserts, "It is unlikely that those beings with few virtuous roots, blessings, karmic affinities can be reborn in the Pure land of the Buddha of

Immeasurable Life and Ultimate Bliss." Our proposal was also made possible by our encounter with Master Shandao's *Commentary on the Contemplation Sutra in Four Fascicles*.

The sentient beings' individual endowments and conditions are evidently the karmic rewards of their good roots and merits. The kind of practice each person prefers, or the type of belief they embrace, shows the path they wish to take. The fact that individuals take different paths means that the karmic rewards and conditions may vary from person to person. Individuals have their particular anticipated conditions for rebirth. Some lean towards rebirth at the time of death, some believe in rebirth through reciting the Buddha's name ten times, and some are convinced that a single thought of yearning for rebirth in Pure land can lead to rebirth after death. How can these differences be reconciled? The paths are diverse, but the goal of liberation is one, requiring such compatibility. The theory of liberation through encounter allows us not to abandon one for the sake of many or to seize one apart from many, but to accept that unity and diversity coexist harmoniously. The karmic rewards of past lives determine the path to liberation in this life, and the varied conditions for rebirth in the Pure land are natural from the perspective of dependent origination. In fact, when Master Shandao describes the favorably encountered practice as "loving and enjoying," he already implies that the karmic rewards of past lives determine the encounters in this life. Our desire and love for a person after our encounter is not determined by our own will. We cannot force ourselves to love someone who does not arouse our desires. When we meet a person and unexpectedly find ourselves in love with the person, we also do not know the reasons behind it. We always fall in love with someone before we justify for the love afterwards. "Love arising with its origin unknown" is one of the essences of love. Love and joy are not determined by our own will nor are they initiated by us. Instead, we are quite passive in the process. My encounter with a person is not determined by my subjective thoughts. Falling in love with a person is also a result of love arising between the person and me, nor is it an action that I decide to initiate. Even the love between parents and children, is not the parents' choice or the child's choice, although seemingly the fact is that parents give birth to the child. The sense of causelessness in love&joy in this life arises from its arising from predetermined conditions, the actions we have done in our unbeginning past lives. We can understand the analogy from this life: if we were forced to learn a musical instrument by our parents when we were young, abandoned it afterwards and later discovered a passionate love for playing that instrument in the adulthood, it precisely illustrates the predetermined nature of love and joy. A child who nearly drowned while playing in the water when they were young, upon reaching adulthood, may forget that experience due to psychological trauma but will forever fear the swimming pool. Both love and aversion, seemingly causeless, are actually predetermined by past deeds that we forgot. The imagery of the Chinese character (pronounced as "Yuan") itself, which translates interdependent origination or condition, also draws our attention. "Yuan" primarily means contact and encounter, and its component part is (sīdài), which means thread, ribbon, or tie. The encounters in this life are guided by a thread, originating from past-life actions, which tie in the end this and that. Using love and joy as a sign for favorable encounter clarifies one of the most perplexing aspect among many practitioners: why would a person persist in a practice unattainable for them? Some believe that sitting in meditation just to Samadhi can lead to liberation, but in today's world, attaining the four dhyānas and eight samādhis is extremely difficult. They themselves acknowledge this, yet they remain unwavering in their pursuit. They also admit that they probably cannot attain the first dhyāna in this life. Should we dissuade them? We can introduce other Dharma ways to them and let them encounter other practices, but it is possible that they are still uninterested in other Dharma ways, not "loving and enjoying" them because they lack what we call "yuan". Of course, it is more likely that they will realize the difficulty and give up, and after having no significant expected progress in their practice, they will turn to other Dharma ways and ultimately attain liberation. Thus, their previous practice of joyfully cultivating meditation was not wasted or useless practice but one of the Dharma ways that as a means, led by detour to another more suitable Dharma way that then lead them to liberation. This also reflects the difference between practice from favorable encounter and love. Loving someone who does not love us in return results in futile efforts, but practicing a Dharma way that we like, even without any expected results, has already planted the seeds of good roots and merits. Therefore, for other practitioners, we should not dissuade or criticize their practice but instead show before them our Dharma way, our practice, and our behavior to them, allowing them to encounter other phenomena. Perhaps they will discover an interest and "joy" in them. It is about demonstration rather than persuasion, about encountering a phenomenon rather than convincing by reasoning. Going with the flow is also appropriate in dealing with others' attitudes.

Therefore, the different criteria for rebirth within the Pure land denomination are all well-founded and correct. We can even say that a person's corresponding karmic rewards will lead to the rebirth criteria they embrace. This does not mean that there are as many rebirth criteria as there are sentient beings. The choice of the Pure land version they believe in is determined by their encounters with people and Dharma. They believe in the rebirth criteria preached by spiritual advisors that they encounter, based on the Pure land scriptures that they preach. Many teachers and spiritual advisors have similar understanding, and there are only a few differing opinions. Therefore, we proclaim what we encounter and agree with, the rebirth conditions and criteria expounded in the *Contemplation Sutra*, which Master Shandao emphasized. One of the main reasons for choosing the *Contemplation Sutra* is that it provides systematic clarification of multiple compatible rebirth conditions and criteria, corresponding to the different endowments and conditions of sentient beings, known as the nine grades of rebirth. Of course, we will also consider and supplement this with the contents of the *Infinite Life Sutra* and the *Amitabha Sutra*. The reason why the topic of liberation through encounter of favorable conditions arises in the *Commentary on the Contemplation Sutra* is that the nine grades of rebirth already imply the idea of liberation by encounter. The practice of rebirth consists of nine grades and conditions, yet the results are the same—rebirth and liberation. Why are there nine different grades of rebirth? It is due to the differences in the conditions of the nine types of ordinary beings. Master Shandao, with keen insight, extended and generalized this concept. Liberation through encounter is a universalization of unity in the diversity that nine grades of rebirth manifests. Thus, the theory of liberation through encounter not only accommodates different opinions within the Pure land but also prevents the possibility of slandering the Dharma. It is also a concept that accommodates the differences in Dharma way practices among all Buddhist denominations and practitioners. However, when it comes to rebirth in Pure land, we still need to look at the various accesses to Pure land practice within the nine grades of rebirth. Our understanding of the *Contemplation Sutra* greatly relies on the commentary of the great knowledgeable master, Master Shandao.

| Class | Grades of rebirth | Mental initiation | Practice method | Practice intensity | Encounter and roots | Difference of fruition |
|---|---|---|---|---|---|---|
| superior | 1st grade: Upper-superior | Those born in the Western Land are of nine grades. Those who attain birth on the highest grade of superior class are sentient beings who resolve to be born in that land, awaken the three kinds of faith, and so are born there. They are, first, sincere faith; second, deep faith; and third, the faith that seeks birth there by transferring one's merit. Those who have these three kinds of faith will certainly be born there. | They are, first, those who have a compassionate heart, abstain from killing, and observe the precepts; second, those who repeat the Mahayana sutras of greater scope; and third, those who practice the six forms of mindfulness. They aspire to be born in that buddha land by transferring there the merit of practice. | With the merit acquired from doing these acts for one to seven days, they attain birth. | Ordinary people of great good with Mahayana tendency. | reaches the insight into the non-arising of all *dharmas*. He is endowed with innumerable hundreds of thousands of *dhāraṇīs*. |
| | 2nd grade: Middle-superior | They have deep faith in the law of karmic cause and effect and do not slight the Mahayana. They aspired to be born in the Land of Utmost Bliss by transferring the merits there. | With fairly good comprehension of Buddha's teachings, they are not dismayed when hearing the supreme truths. They aspired to be born in the Land of Utmost Bliss by transferring the merits there. | No particular act is required | Ordinary people of middle good with Mahayana tendency. | After seven days, he immediately reaches the stage of non-retrogression for realizing highest, perfect enlightenment. |
| | 3rd grade: Lower-superior | accept the law of karmic cause and effects | Do not speak slightly of the Mahayana, and awaken aspiration for highest enlightenment. They transfer the merit acquired to the Land of Utmost Bliss, aspiring to be born there | No particular act is required except to have one single thought to aspire for the highest enlightenment. | Ordinary people of lesser good with Mahayana tendency. | After three smaller *kalpas* he acquires clear understanding of the one hundred *dharmas* and dwells in the stage of joy. |

| Class | Grades of rebirth | Mental initiation | Practice method | Practice intensity | Encounter and roots | Difference of fruition |
|---|---|---|---|---|---|---|
| Medium | 4th grade: Upper-medium | The sentient beings who keep the five precepts, observe the eight abstinences, practice in compliance with various precepts, and abstain from committing the five heinous offenses and other transgressions. | They transfer the merit acquired to the Western Land of Utmost Bliss, aspiring to be born there | The duration is lifelong according to Shandao | Ordinary people of great good with Hinayana tendency | When the flower blossoms, he immediately attains arhatship, acquires the three kinds of transcendent knowledge and the six supernatural powers, and realizes the eight *samādhis* of liberation. |
| | 5th grade: Middle-medium | the sentient beings who observe for at least a day and a night the eight abstinences, the precepts for a novice, or the complete precepts of a monk or a nun, and do not violate any of the rules of conduct. | They transfer the merit acquired to the Land of Utmost Bliss, aspiring to be born there. | The duration of observance of precepts is a day and a night | Ordinary people of middle good with Hinayana tendency | After half a *kalpa*, he becomes an arhat. |
| | 6th grade: Lower-medium | virtuous men and women who are dutiful to and care for their parents and do benevolent deeds for others. | He may meet a good teacher, who fully explains to him the bliss of the land of Amitāyus and the Forty-eight Great Vows of Bhikṣu Dharmākara. | receive good spiritual advisor | Ordinary people of lesser good with Hinayana tendency | Seven days after his birth there, he reaches the stage of stream-winner. After one smaller *kalpa*, he becomes an arhat. |

| Class | Grades of rebirth | Mental initiation | Practice method | Practice intensity | Encounter and roots | Difference of fruition |
|---|---|---|---|---|---|---|
| inferior | 7th grade: Upper-inferior | They commit various evil acts but do not slander the Mahayana sutras of greater scope. When a foolish person such as this, who has committed much evil but feels no remorse | he may meet a good teacher, who praises the titles of the twelve divisions of the Mahayana scriptures. Furthermore, this wise teacher advises him to join his palms and call, 'Homage to Amitāyus Buddha'. (Na mo Amitabha) | receive good spiritual advisor at the ending stage of their life. | Ordinary people of lesser sin | In seven weeks the lotus bud blossoms. After ten smaller *kalpas*, he acquires clear understanding of the one hundred *dharmas* and enters the first stage of a Bodhisattva. |
| | 8th grade: Middle-inferior | The sentient beings who violate the five precepts, the eight precepts, or the complete precepts of a monk or a nun. A foolish person remorselessly steals from the sangha, or takes the personal belongings of monks, or preaches the Dharma with impure motives | receive a good teacher, who compassionately explains to him the ten supernal powers of Amitāyus, fully describing the majestic power of the light of that buddha and his virtues in the observance of the precepts, meditation, wisdom, liberation, and knowledge of liberation. | receive a good spiritual advisor | Ordinary people of middle sin violating precepts | After six *kalpas* the lotus bud blossoms. Upon hearing Mahayana truth, he immediately awakens aspiration for highest enlightenment. |
| | 9th grade: Lower-inferior | the sentient beings who commit five heinous offenses, the ten evil acts, and various immoral acts. | receive a good teacher who teaches him the wonderful Dharma, urging him to be mindful of the Buddha; The teacher then advises him, 'If you cannot concentrate on the Buddha then you should say instead, "Homage to Amitāyus Buddha."' So he sincerely and continuously says, 'Homage to Amitāyus Buddha' ten times. (Na Mo Amitabha) | receive a good spiritual advisor and recite Na Mo Amitabha for ten times. | Ordinary people of immense sin committing five heinous offenses. | After twelve great *kalpas*, the lotus bud blossoms. He rejoices and immediately awakens aspiration for highest enlightenment. |

Chapter

# 2

*The Contemplation Sutra* and the
Nine Grades of Rebirth

## 2.1  *The Contemplation Sutra* and Ordinary Beings

Among the three Pure land sutras, *The Contemplation Sutra* holds a special position because its intended audience is a laywoman named Vaidehi, an ordinary person. Initially, the Buddha taught her the Samadhi of Visualization of Buddha, as she is one of ordinary beings who possess the conditions for meditative concentration. Subsequently, without the request of those present, the Buddha expounded the conditions and details of rebirth in the Pure land, known as the Nine Grades of Rebirth, for ordinary people to attain liberation. "The Samadhi of Buddha-visualization originates from Vaidehi's request, while the discourse on the Nine Grades of Rebirth is expounded directly from the Buddha himself from his own initiative without the request of others." In the *Infinite Life Sutra*, the assembly of listeners are Bodhisattvas, and the one requesting the teaching is venerable Ananda. The discourse aims to benefit humans, heavenly beings, and Bodhisattvas by explaining the formation of the Pure land. In the *Amitabha Sutra*, the discourse is directed to a group of monks led by the arhat Shariputra. Each sutra is targeted at its particular audience, and thus, the Buddha's Pure land rebirth teachings vary from one sutra to another. We do not shun the difference of teachings on rebirth attainment among the three Pure land Sutras. In *Amitabha Sutra* the Buddha says that by repeating the name of Buddha Amitabha in the span of one day to sevens with single mindedness one can attain Pure land; whereas in the *Contemplation Sutra* the Buddha says that with ten times repeating of the Amitabha Buddha, the person can be reborn in one of the nine grades.

Regarding ordinary people, the target of *The Contemplation Sutra*, Master Shandao clarifies the point of apparent conflict caused by people who believe in other Sutras and dissuade the believer of the *Contemplation Sutra* from their faith of certified rebirth after this life. He explains that these practitioners may use scriptural references to argue against the possibility of rebirth to the person in question. In response, ordinary beings like him will reply, "Even if the venerable ones present scriptural references to prove that I cannot attain rebirth, I will firmly adhere to my belief. Why? Not that I do not trust those scriptures. I respect and believe in them all. However, when the Buddha expounded those scriptures, they were spoken in different contexts, at different times, and for different audiences, addressing different needs and benefits, the occasions were different. At that time, the Buddha expounded the methods for sentient beings including ordinary people, heavenly beings, and Bodhisattvas. Now, he is teaching the Samadhi of Buddha Recitation and the cultivation of virtuous practices for all ordinary beings like Vaidehi and others, who are troubled by the Five Defilements and Five Sufferings in the post-Buddha era, to attain rebirth. In reliance on these circumstances, I wholeheartedly abide by the teachings of this Buddha Dharma in this Sutra."

As ordinary beings, we primarily rely on *The Contemplation Sutra*. Master Shandao's explanation points out the uniqueness of this sutra specifically tailored for ordinary beings in the Dharma Ending Age. However, this does not mean that the method of single-minded, undistracted repeating of Amitabha Buddha as taught in the *Amitabha Sutra* contradicts the teachings of *The Contemplation Sutra*. In the next chapter, we will explore an alternative interpretation of single-mindedness in various translations of the *Amitabha Sutra*, which harmonizes with the truth of Pure land as explained in *The Contemplation Sutra*. For now, we can conclude that the possibility of rebirth depends on our positioning among the Nine Grades and whether we receive the rebirth conditions specified for each grade. Whether we can attain rebirth in accordance with *The Contemplation Sutra* depends on faith and aspiration, while the quantity and quality of Buddha recitation determine the grade. At the beginning of this chapter, I have listed a table of the Nine Grades of Rebirth based on *The Contemplation Sutra* for readers' reference.

In the history of Chinese Pure land Buddhism, except for a few masters like Master Shandao, the concept of the Nine Grades of Rebirth has been largely neglected. In the Nine Grades of Rebirth, it is explicitly stated that as long as one aspires to be reborn in the Pure land, the practice can be simplified to repeating Amitabha Buddha's name only ten times, and one will attain rebirth. For ordinary beings who believe in the Hinayana teachings, rebirth can be achieved by dedicating their precepts to the Pure land. For Buddhist practitioners who follow Mahayana teachings, rebirth can be attained by dedicating the merits of reciting Mahayana scriptures to the Pure land. Even for an ordinary being who commits great evil, rebirth can be attained by reciting "Namo Amitabha Buddha" ten times at the moment of death. In the context of the superior grades of rebirth, which apply to practitioners of Mahayana and Hinayana, repeating does not merely refer to the conventional meaning of repeating Buddha's name but instead refers to the thought of being reborn in the Pure land, dedicating one's good deeds to the Pure land, and fulfilling this practice to achieve the superior grades of rebirth. This may challenge the conventional understanding of Pure land practice prevalent since the Southern Song Dynasty, but the sutra itself and Master Shandao's commentary unequivocally point out the key aspects of Pure land practice.

## 2.2 The Structure of *The Contemplation Sutra*

*The Contemplation Sutra* can be divided into four parts structurally. The traditional preface narrates a complete story of queen Vaidehi's unfortunate sufferings during a political coup. This leads to Vaidehi to the Buddha who taught her the Samadhi Visualization of Buddha. Being imprisoned after the coup and nearly killed by her own son, Vaidehi is tired of her role as a queen and desires to be reborn in a place free from worries, evils or harsh words. As a Buddhist, she implores the Buddha to "teach her to contemplate on pure practices" and "teach her to think of right receptivity," which refers to a practice of Samadhi, leading to the so-called 13 contemplations and its visualization. This marks the first part of the Authentic Teaching section, where the Buddha immediately demonstrates and explains the Samadhi of visualization of Buddha, it is known as the "good Samadhi karma", or concentrated good deeds. This section serves as a detailed manual for the practice of achieving the Samadhi visualization of Buddha. After teaching the thirteenth visualization, which focuses on how to contemplate the Bodhisattva Mahasthamaprapta, the Buddha concludes the answers that Vaidehi requires. Vaidehi's identity as an ordinary being, along with the worldly causes and conditions that made her suffer, is noteworthy. This clearly indicates that *The Contemplation Sutra* is directed towards ordinary beings. Vaidehi represents ordinary beings, and today we resonate with her situation—discord among family members, struggles for power, and the impermanence of worldly affairs, etc.

The second section is the teachings on the nine grades of rebirth, which is entirely dedicated to the rebirth of ordinary beings who are incapable of practicing the Samadhi visualization of Buddha. This part is known as "scattered good deeds". Master Shandao explains, "The passages on the nine grades of rebirth are not requested by anyone at the presence of Buddha; the Buddha spontaneously gives the teaching". After the teachings on the nine grades of rebirth, the authentic teachings conclude, leaving the remaining section as the distribution part.

It is crucial to note that the Samadhi Visualization of Buddha, represented by the thirteen visualization, is not a necessary condition for rebirth. The reasons for the Buddha's instruction on the Samadhi visualization of Buddha are stated as: "To teach Queen Vaidehi and all future beings to contemplate the Western Pure land, through the power of the Buddha, and upon seeing that Pure land, just as if holding a bright mirror before them, they will see its reflections, and upon seeing the wondrous and delightful aspects of that land, their minds will become joyful, thereby immediately attaining the patient rest in belief in immortality". After Pure land was brought to the view of Queen Vaidehi through the Buddha's superpower, her following question, "Encumbered by defiled evil and the five sufferings, how can I see Amitabha Buddha's Western Pure land?" Thus, the Buddha instructed her the way to visualize Pure land based on observable phenomena in this world. This means that Vaidehi is not satisfied merely with seeing Pure land through Buddha Shakyamuni's power, but she wishes to see the Pure land at her own initiative, so that the image seen can always give her joy. That is the reason that the Buddha teaches her how to visualize the Pure land.

Although the thirteen visualization are all excellent methods for attaining rebirth and dispelling karmic hindrances, the main focus in *Contemplation Sutra* is the teachings on the nine grades of rebirth. While the thirteen contemplations are indeed aimed at ordinary beings, for those ordinary beings who possess the conditions for meditation practice, it should be clarified that their main purpose is not for rebirth but to *see* the Western Pure land in this lifetime. The nine grades of rebirth, on the other hand, are intended for ordinary beings without the conditions for meditation practice, offering various methods for *rebirth* in the Western Pure land. Thus, when studying the *Contemplation Sutra*, we should stress the teachings of the nine grades of rebirth.

Regarding the relationship between rebirth and the Samadhi visualization of Buddha Amitabha, the Buddha distinguishes between "Good Karma" and "Pure Karma". "Good Karma" refers to the practices required for rebirth in the Pure land, such as filial piety towards parents, taking refuge in the Three Jewels, deep belief in karma, and reciting Mahayana sutras, corresponding to the high and Middle classes of Rebirth in the Nine Grades. On the other hand, "Pure Karma" represents the result of the practice of the thirteen visualization, allowing one to see the Pure land. These two are clearly different. Master Shandao is unambiguous about the relationship between rebirth and the Samadhi visualization of Buddha: rebirth does not necessarily require proficiency in the Samadhi contemplation of Buddha. He says, "Three types of sentient beings can attain rebirth. Who are these three? First, those who can maintain precepts and cultivate compassion; second, those who cannot maintain precepts and cultivate compassion but can read and recite Mahayana sutras; third, those who cannot maintain precepts, read sutras, but can only recite the names of Buddha, Dharma, and Sangha. These three types of individuals, according to their own karma, concentrate diligently for one day and one night, or up to seven days and seven nights continuously, and seek rebirth. When their lives come to an end, Amitabha Buddha and the assembly of transformed Buddhas and Bodhisattvas will emit light and extend their hands, and in the blink of an eye, they will be reborn in that land." The teaching of the Three Pure Rewarding Karmas comes before the introduction of the thirteen visualization. Master Shandao mentions, "The Buddha further observes and reveals the performance of the three pure rewarding karmas." The relationship between the three rewarding karmas and the thirteen contemplations is that "All sentient beings can be classified into two types: those who have conditions for meditative concentration and those without. For those who rely on meditative concentration, they can attain birth in the Pure land according to the instruction of 13 visualization. But this does not cover all sentient beings, therefore, the Tathagata, out of expedient means, reveals and expounds the three rewarding karmas suitable to those who can only make various scattered good deeds."

Thus, the thirteen visualization in the *The Contemplation Sutra* is taught to those who have the conditions and abilities for meditative concentration, while the three rewarding karmas and the Nine Grades of Rebirth are for ordinary beings who can only engage in scattered practices. From Vaidehi's situation, we can also understand why the Buddha taught the visualization Samadhi. Vaidehi first wanted to see the Pure land, and secondly, she was a noblewoman imprisoned due to circumstances, indicating that she had the conditions for meditation. In conclusion, as most of today's ordinary people lack the conditions for meditation in the Dharma Ending Age, because of lack of personal talent and lack of supporting circumstances for meditation, plus that the visualization of Buddha is not the decisive practice for rebirth, our focus on interpreting *The Contemplation Sutra* lies in the section on the Nine Grades of Rebirth.

## 2.3 The Differentiated Classes of Rebirth and the Nine Grades of Rebirth in the Pure land

After answering Vaidehi's question about how to be reborn in the Pure land with the Thirteen Visualization, the Buddha said, "People to be reborn into the Western Pure land can be classified into nine grades." We know that the rebirth falls into three major classes (superior, medium, inferior), each respectively divided further into three subcategories, totaling nine grades. Why does the matter of rebirth have nine different types or levels? Master Shandao explains, "Examine the intent of the various passages in *the Contemplation Sutra*, and it is all about how after the Buddha's passing, ordinary beings, though defiled, differ in the encounters that lead to the nine grades." Here, we can see Master Shandao's thought of liberation through encounter once again. In fact, the classification of the nine grades of rebirth is the most specific embodiment of liberation by encounter.

The nine grades are classified into three classes from superior to inferior. The three classes differ in terms of the encounters of conditions that lead to rebirth. Master Shandao continues to explain, "The superior class consists of those who encounter great favorable conditions, the medium one consists of those who encounter lesser favorable conditions, and the inferior one consists of those who are in evil conditions." The superior class consists of ordinary beings who encounter Mahayana practitioners, the medium class consists of those who encounter Theravada practitioners, and the inferior one consists of ordinary beings who are evil-doers. It is due to these differences in encounters that each group of rebirth are divided further into the upper, middle, and lower grades. It is important to note that their rebirth is not based on their accomplishment in Mahayana or Theravada or their good or evil deeds. Instead, all of them aspire to be born in Amitabha's Pure land by dedicating the merits of their good deeds or the recitation of "Namo Amitabha Buddha" upon death. The driving force behind all rebirths is the power of Amitabha Buddha's fulfilled vows.

In the *Commentary on the Contemplation Sutra*, Master Shandao explains the nine grades of rebirth twice. In Volume One, he first refutes the idea proposed by some scholars that the first six of the nine grades correspond to the six staged attainments of the holy ones. In Volume Four, he details the nine grades of rebirth for the second time. The meaning in both explanations is essentially the same; the difference lies only in the degree of detailing.

Now, let us examine the Master Shandao's outline of the nine grades of rebirth in Volume One of his commentary. To depict the various types of ordinary beings within the superior class, he first explains the upper-superior, middle-superior, and lower-superior grades. First, we need to understand that encountering great ordinary beings refers to encountering Mahayana practitioners who believe in Mahayana Buddhism. It does not necessarily mean that they have already attained great achievements through Mahayana practice. The upper superior rebirth contains two types of individuals: the first type relies on initiatives based on the Three Minds (or three faiths), namely the utmost Sincere Mind, the Profound Mind, and the Aspiration and merits-transferring Mind, to be reborn; the second type consists of three kinds of sentient beings. Traditional Pure land interpretations often focus on the Three Minds, but we will discuss them later. In Master Shandao's explanation of the upper superior class of rebirth, he particularly emphasizes the three kinds of sentient beings:

"Three types of sentient beings attain rebirth. What are these three? First, those who can maintain precepts and cultivate compassion; second, those who cannot maintain precepts but can recite Mahayana sutras; third, those who cannot maintain precepts or recite sutras, but can only recite the name of Buddha, Dharma, and Sangha. These three types wish to transfer merits of their own karma to the rebirth in Pure land, concentrate on the desire and ideas to be born in Pure land, continuously and diligently for a day and a night, maintain it to one or to seven days. At the end of their lives, Amitabha Buddha and the assembly of transformed Buddhas and Bodhisattvas will appear before them, and they will be reborn in the Pure land in an instant."

Seemingly Master Shandao merely restates the sutra's text, "Three types of sentient beings will attain rebirth. Who are they precisely? First, those who are compassionate and who refrain from killing, adhering to various precepts; second, those who recite and uphold various Mahayana scriptures; third, those who practice the six recollections and dedicate their merits to rebirth in the western Buddha's land. With these merits, they will attain rebirth in one to seven days." It is essential to note that in Master Shandao's summary of the three types of sentient beings, he emphasizes that these three types of behaviors have a *disjunctive* relationship. It does not mean that a person must maintain precepts, cultivate compassion, recite Mahayana sutras, and recite the names of Buddha, Dharma, and Sangha all at once. Instead, it means that if one does maintain precepts and cultivate compassion but does not recite Mahayana sutras, or if one recites Mahayana sutras but does not maintain precepts, or if one practices only the six recollections without doing the other two, as long as they persist in one of these three behaviors for one to seven days, they can dedicate the merits generated from this behavior to rebirth and attain the superior class of rebirth.

Those in the middle superior grade need to "deeply believe in cause and effect, without slandering Mahayana Buddhism, and with this good root, vow to be reborn". The correspondent text in the sutra for this class is, "Those in the middle superior grade do not need to uphold and recite various Mahayana sutras, but they have excellent understanding of the teachings, their minds are not disturbed regarding the meaning of primary first principle, and they deeply believe in cause and effect without slandering Mahayana." Why is there "no need of upholding and reciting various Mahayana sutras?" "Why is there 'no need'? It is not about whether one recites or not; it is about good understanding of and faith in the Mahayana teachings." In other words, as long as they have understanding of and faith in the teachings of Mahayana without actually reciting the sutras, they, as a result of their good roots and dedication, attain the middle superior grade of rebirth. As for ordinary individuals in the lower superior class, they need only "not slander Mahayana and have the intention for the unsurpassed enlightenment. This one thought is considered the right good practice needed for the rebirth; apart from this, no other good practices are needed. Seeking rebirth in this way, at the end of their lives, they will be immediately received by Amitabha Buddha and the assembly of transformed Buddhas and Bodhisattvas before they attain rebirth." The correspondent sentence in the Sutra is: "The lower superior grade rebirth is attained by those having faith in cause and effect, refraining from slandering Mahayana teachings, and having the aspiration for the unsurpassed enlightenment." Master Shandao emphasizes that achieving the lower superior grade of rebirth is solely based on not slandering Mahayana teachings and developing the aspiration for supreme enlightenment. Nowadays, followers of Mahayana Buddhism may find it difficult to understand why refraining from slandering Mahayana teachings is mentioned as a particular *virtue*. It is essential to comprehend that in the time when Mahayana Buddhist doctrines were first declared, the followers of Shakyamuni Buddha initially entered Buddhism through the Theravada tradition, such that when they encounter Mahayana teachings, many feel bewildered and troubled as it conflicts with their own past Theravada beliefs. Therefore, understanding Mahayana without slandering its teachings and not clinging to Theravada is considered a virtue. For all three superior grades and ordinary individuals are just Buddhist followers who understand and believe in Mahayana Buddhism, they are classified as 'ordinary people encountering the great favorable conditions', the latter designating Mahayana Buddhist doctrines. We tend to ask questions: since superior grade are all reborn in the Pure land, Why is it classified further into three levels? Actually the further division into three levels differs in the *How* of the beings are received by Amitabha Buddha.

Master Shandao observed: "*When those of the upper superior ascend to the Pure land, Amitabha Buddha and an assembly of innumerable transformed Buddhas extend their hands to the person simultaneously. When those of the middle superior ascend, Amitabha Buddha and a thousand transformed Buddhas extend their hands. When those of the lower superior grade ascend, Amitabha Buddha and five hundred transformed Buddhas extend their hands. These differences result from their karma, strong or weak. The second distinction among the superior three grades are the varied speed of progress in seeing the Buddha, hearing the Dharma, and achieving irreversible enlightenment among the three grades. Additionally, there are differences of the time interval of individuals, after attaining non-retrogression, can return as compassionate guides to rescue suffering beings outside the Pure land."*

Now, let us look at the three grades of rebirth within the medium class. It designates people who are classified as those who encounter less favorable conditions, which means people who are concerned of their own liberation only, namely Hinayna Buddhist believers. For those in the upper medium grade, they are described as those who "observe the Five Precepts and Eight Precepts, diligently practice all precepts without committing the Five Heinous Acts, and are free from major transgressions. When they are close to death, Amitabha Buddha and the assembly of monastic disciples emit light and appear before them, allowing them to attain rebirth instantly." These individuals adhered to the precepts of the Lesser Vehicle after Shakyamuni Buddha disappears from this world. Master Shandao summarizes those in the lower grade of the middle class as "ordinary beings after the Buddha's passing, who, with less virtuous roots, are given Hinayana precepts by someone they encounter, and they dedicate their merits to be reborn." In the middle medium grade are individuals who vow to observe the precepts for one day and one night, aspiring for rebirth in the Pure land. When they are close to death and see the Buddha, they attain rebirth immediately. These individuals are described by Master Shandao as "ordinary beings without virtues who, after encountering minor favorable conditions and being taught the Lesser Vehicle precepts for a day and night, aspire for rebirth, and through the power of Buddha's vows, achieve rebirth." From the first two types of individuals in the medium class, we can understand why Master Shandao calls those in the middle grade 'ordinary individuals who encounter less favorable conditions'. It refers to those who come across the Lesser Vehicle teachings and encounter good advisors of the Lesser Vehicle. It does not mean individuals who have achieved something great in their Hinayana practice, nor does it refer to 'professional' practitioners strictly adhering to the Lesser Vehicle practice to a certain level. Those in the middle-middle grade only need to observe the precepts for one day and one night to attain rebirth. Master Shandao specifically clarifies that before they come across the Lesser Vehicle and observe the precepts for a day and night, they are ordinary people without virtues.

Now we turn our regard to the lower class of rebirth. In the 6th grade are even ordinary people who are not

Buddhists. 'If there are sentient beings who practice filial piety and compassion, and at the time of death, they encounter good advisors who speak of the joys and forty-eight vows of that Buddha's Pure land, upon hearing it, they will be born in that land.' Master Shandao summarizes them as 'those who, even though they only perform worldly good acts such as filial piety and do not have the intention to seek liberation in this life, but they are motivated by the good advice they hear at the time of death, which leads them to generate the aspiration for rebirth, they will be reborn in the Pure land '. These individuals in the lower grade of the middle class do *not* have Buddhist belief , they have knowledge neither of the Mahayana nor Lesser Vehicle teachings. They are simply nice people considered in terms of secular standards. Their motivation to seek rebirth in the Pure land is not driven by Mahayana's aspiration to save sentient beings or Lesser Vehicle's motivation to attain personal liberation from afflictions. Instead, they hope to escape the suffering of the Six Realms and dedicate the worldly merits they accumulated towards rebirth in the Pure land, thus attaining the rebirth in the 6th grade. Of course, readers may have questions about why these individuals, who are just ordinary people with secular interests, are categorized as 'ordinary individuals who encounter the Lesser Vehicle' by Shandao as well. The reason is that their motivation for rebirth in Amitabha's Pure land is merely to transcend this suffering world (Samsara) after this life, in other words, to seek the 'bliss' part of the Pure land. The good advisors they encounter at the time of death 'extensively explain the joys of living at Amitabha Buddha's Pure land. This motivation is quite similar to the aspiration for liberation from birth and death held by followers of the Lesser Vehicle which concern only their *own* liberation. After those people with secular interests being born in the Pure land, they attain the fruit of Sotapanna and subsequently become Arhats.

We can see that for the first two classes, the six grades are arranged like a gradually descending staircase based on the strength of merits. The merits associated with Mahayana Buddhism are greater than those associated with Hinayana Buddhism, and both are greater than worldly merits. These merits are general secular virtues that laypeople can spontaneously act, and they are not related to the cultivation of Samadhi (meditative concentration) and Prajna (wisdom of emptiness) attained through specialized monastic practices. The six first grades are arranged according to the strength of merits, and those who have no merits whatsoever fall into the category 'doer of evil'.

The inferior three grades consist of ordinary beings who have committed various degrees of evils. The text describes them as "having no roots of goodness in either Buddhist teachings or secular actions; they know nothing except doing evils." In the 7th grade of rebirth are people who "have committed evils but have not slandered the Dharma. They neither feel shameful or regretful for the evils done, but at the moment of death, when they encounter good spiritual teachers who speak of Mahayana Buddhism and instruct them to recite the name of Buddha only once, Amitabha Buddha will send Avalokiteshvara Bodhisattva to receive them, and they will be reborn in the Pure land." The reason why even evil people attain rebirth in the Pure land simply by reciting the Buddha's name once is that at the moment of death, they encounter good spiritual teachers who praise the titles of the twelve Mahayana sutras, and upon hearing these titles, they have their extremely heavy evil karmas accumulated over thousands of kalpas eliminated. This shows that whether one recites sutra titles or the Buddha's name, the effect is the same as long as they dedicate the merits for the rebirth to Pure land, which will lead to actual rebirth afterwards. Just as in the case of the highest grade of Mahayana rebirth, reciting and dedicating the merits of reading Mahayana scriptures leads to rebirth. However, readers may wonder what differentiates the rebirth of evil people from that of virtuous people. Evil people reborn in the lower grade of the Pure land first stay in the lotus flower for forty-nine days before formal entrance in the Pure land. This period, like further development in the womb, lasts much longer than people of other grades. To reach the stage of beginning Bodhisattvas, they need to go through ten small kalpas for they are on the threshhold in cultivation. Those in the lower grade of the middle class, however, in just one small kalpa, become Arhats, while those in the middle grade of the high grade achieve the position of Anagamis, which in Mahayana corresponds to the seventh stage of Bodhisattva. However, these distinctions of time dimensions after entering the Pure land are not important for us ordinary people in this world; what is important is going to the Pure land after death. In fact, the first seven grades already include the vast majority of ordinary beings, including those who believe in Hinayana, those who believe in Mahayana, ordinary virtuous people, and ordinary evil people. The individuals of 7th grade are all, in the worldly sense, evil people, and Master Shandao refers to them as "evil individuals that we see everywhere." This shows the broad scope of the Pure land's salvation. However, there are still two kinds of evil doers who have committed sinful karma beyond worldly evil but they can be reborn in the Pure land. These are the apostates of Buddhism in the 8th grade and the ordinary beings in the low grade of the inferior class who have committed the grave five heinous offenses. The individuals in the 8th grade include those who "initially accepted the Buddhist precepts, but later either damaged or violated them completely; who also stole items from the Sangha and presented them as their own; who preached the impure Dharma, without the slightest sense of shame or regret." These are the worms and heretics within Buddhism. When these individuals encounter good spiritual teachers who expound the merits of the Pure land, they will attain rebirth in the 8th grade. Finally, the individuals in the lower grade of the inferior class are those who "have committed evil deeds, the five heinous offenses, and the ten evil acts; who are full of various evils; who, due to their evil karma, are bound to degrade into hell for many kalpas; who, at the time of death, encounter good spiritual teachers who teach them to recite the name of Amitabha Buddha and urge them to seek rebirth, they will be reborn by reciting the Buddha's name." Thus, we can see that, based on the nine grades, those who believe in Mahayana, those who believe in Hinayana, those who do good worldly deeds, those who do evil worldly deeds, those who break Buddhist precepts, those who commit grave evil deeds, are all embraced by the Pure land's rebirth approach. All ordinary beings them are qualified for rebirth; the only condition is to believe in the existence of the Pure land and aspire to be reborn there. Therefore, Master Shandao refers to the nine grades of rebirth as embracing all beings, regardless of whether they are great or small mortal beings, whether they are virtuous or evil in terms of deeds done. These nine grades *encompass all ordinary human beings*. We should take note of the motivation for the rebirth of the evil individuals. They are different from those whose motivation starts from believing in Mahayana, who aspire to cultivate as Bodhisattvas, or those who believe in Hinayana, who aspire to attain the position of Arhats. The motivation of evil individuals in the inferior class is merely to escape the sight of hell at the moment of death. At this precise moment, someone by their side speaks about the merits of the Pure land, inspiring them to seek rebirth, they, only for the reason to evade the inevitable fall into the hell, are reborn by the power of the vow of Amitabha Buddha. "To these sinful individuals, due to their evil karma, they should fall into hell, and at the moment of death, the flames of hell will all arise. When they encounter good spiritual teachers with great compassion who praise Amitabha Buddha's ten powers and majestic virtues, extol the Buddha's radiant divine powers, and also praise the virtues of precepts, samadhi, wisdom, liberation, and the knowledge and views of liberation, once these individuals hear this, they will be relieved of the sins of countless kalpas. The fierce fires of hell will be transformed into cool breezes, scattering heavenly flowers in all directions. These flowers will give rise to countless transformation Buddhas and Bodhisattvas who will receive these individuals, and in an instant, they will be reborn within the seven-jeweled pond and lotus flower." As the nine grades of rebirth actually encompass all sentient beings who wish to be reborn and believe they will be reborn, there is no difference between virtuous and evil individuals in terms of whether they can be reborn in the Pure land. There is also no difference between arriving early or late in the Pure land; once any sentient being enters the Pure land, they will naturally experience bliss and liberation. This concludes the overview of the nine grades of rebirth in the Pure land.

## 2.4 Rebirth and the Grades of Rebirth

The inclusion of the inferior three grades, consisting of evil ordinary beings, in the nine grades of rebirth may seem contrary to the conventional understanding of traditional Pure land Buddhism. Traditional Pure land teachings often encourage people to recite the Buddha's name as frequently as people can because, from a common understanding of justice, it might seem fair and reasonable that if a person does good deeds and recites the Buddha's name in their lifetime, they will attain rebirth. On the other hand, if a person does evil deeds and only recites "Namo Amitabha Buddha" at the end of their life, it might appear unfair for them to attain rebirth. If rebirth is so easy to attain, why do other people need to continue reciting the Buddha's name?

These doubts arise from viewing rebirth through a

worldly and secular perspective, trying to measure Buddha's compassion with conventional norms. The compassion of Amitabha Buddha is boundless, transcending the limitations of worldly understanding. The amount of Buddha-name recitation and whether one attains rebirth are not based on a transactional relationship. Amitabha Buddha's vows clearly state that all sentient beings who hear His name, take refuge in Him, and aspire for rebirth will be embraced and supported by His compassionate vows. The quantity of Buddha-name recitation is only related to the grade of rebirth which only has some difference in terms of time of accomplishment after attaining rebirth, not the principle of whether one can attain rebirth or not.

The seemingly unconventional idea that evil individuals can be reborn in the Pure land with just a few recitations of the Buddha's name can be explained by understanding the concept of "liberation by encounter" in both this and past lifetimes. Even if an ordinary being committed grave offenses like the Five Heinous Crimes, if they encounter someone explaining the virtues of the Pure land at the time of death and wish to be reborn there, it indicates that they had accumulated merits and karmic affinities with the

Pure land in their past lifetimes, enabling them to receive a virtuous teacher at the time of death and to be reborn there. Master Shandao emphasized that "One cannot attain rebirth in that Buddha's land without some virtuous roots and blessings." The nine grades of rebirth encompass various individuals, all of whom have accumulated significant merits. While their present life circumstances differ, they all encounter the Dharma of the Pure land, and thus, they will be reborn there. Although there are differences among the nine grades of rebirth, all of them have encountered the Dharma way of the Pure land, indicating that they have accumulated significant merits. They all have common points in their predestined connections with the Pure land, leading to their rebirth. The difference lies in the specific encounters they have in this life, some encountering Mahayana teachings, others encountering Theravada teachings, and some have evil influences during most of their lives but receive ultimately good teachers, resulting in the variation of grade.

The nine grades of ordinary beings can be divided into two categories: good and evil, representing the distinction between the high six grades and the lower three grades, and Mahayana and Theravada beliefs, representing the difference between the high three grades and the middle three grades. However, in reality, after attaining rebirth in the Pure land, those in the high three grades and the lower three grades will eventually attain Mahayana, and the categories of good and evil and Mahayana and Theravada together encompass the nine grades of rebirth. Whether one is a good or evil person in this life is mainly determined by their predestined connections in past lives, just as whether one prefers Mahayana or Theravada Buddhism is determined by their past lives. In the context of the nine grades of rebirth, the distinction between those with Mahayana or Theravada tendencies is respected by Amitabha Buddha. Those in the 4th grade of the middle class will attain Arhatship upon reaching the Pure land, while those in the 5th grade will attain the level of Srotaapanna after seven days, and those in the 6th grade will attain the level of Srotaapanna after a small kalpa.

It is not the case, as in popular belief, that everyone who enters the Pure land ultimately becomes Bodhisattvas or Buddhas. Many will attain Arhatship, and the Amitabha Sutra also mentions that there are many Arhats in the Pure land. The three types of evil ordinary beings in the lower grade will undergo practice and develop the Bodhi mind within the Pure land. Although they were extremely evil, they will eventually become Mahayana accomplished beings. This is because, at the time of their death, they encounter good teachers who expound the merits of Mahayana sutras and teachings, which can extinguish their heavy evil karma. Only Mahayana sutras possess such powerful merits, and their evil actions in this life become the bridge connecting them to the Mahayana teachings. These somewhat counter-intuitive points demonstrate that the distinction between Mahayana and Theravada practitioners remains even when people enter the Pure land and transform their "souls" and physical bodies. This distinction is determined by the differences in their predestined connections in past lives and their motivations, aspirations in this life, these factors determine whether they are sentient beings with Mahayana or Theravada tendencies.

Moreover, as we accept the idea of nine grades of rebirth, attaining rebirth in the Pure land is so easy that one existential question that Pure land believers often confront has a suitable response, if not an answer. We can resume the question in the following formula: given that rebirth in Pure land only depends on continuous repeating of the Amitabha's name according traditional interpretation, why not commit suicide while repeating it to ensure rebirth for the maximum certitude? This question is resolved by understanding the excellence of the nine grades of rebirth and change the given of the question. Because rebirth in the Pure land is so easy and assured according to nine grades, one does not need to resort to suicide to secure rebirth for its certitude. Even an evil person, when their life comes to an end, can be reborn by hearing Amitabha's name from someone. People need not consider suicide to attain rebirth as an option. The Dharma of Amitabha Buddha does not adhere to conventional notions of fairness because the Buddha's vow power and compassion are inconceivable; he does not abandon anyone, even if they have done extremely evil deeds. This may blur the clear distinction between good and evil in terms of karmic retribution for good people, but Amitabha Buddha's fundamental vow is to save all beings, and "those who can recite his name even once, from ten times upwards, will all be reborn through the power of the Buddha's vow." This may blur the clear distinction between good and evil in terms of karmic retribution for people, but

Amitabha Buddha's fundamental vow is to save all beings regardless of their history. The unsurpassable compassion and the power of the vow of Amitabha is not to be measured by worldly understanding.

Traditional Pure land teachings encourage proficiency in repeating the Buddha's name and approaching certain meditative state, the Samadhi of contemplation of Amitabha, as ideal practice for Pure land believers. However, there is no basis for this in the Contemplation Sutra or in the commentary of it by Shandao. The elevation of rebirth in terms of ranking of grade depends on the level of motivation, whether Mahayana or Theravada, while rebirth itself depends on the strength of faith and aspiration. With the conviction and aspiration for rebirth, one can be reborn in the Pure land without relying on the proficiency of Buddha-name repeating. Various forms of meritorious practices, including virtuous deeds, observance of precepts, recitation of the Buddha's name, and repeating of Mahayana scriptures, are all conducive to rebirth as long as one dedicate them for rebirth in Pure land. Amitabha Buddha's acceptance of beings does not depend on how diligently or proficiently one repeats his name. Amitabha

Buddha's vow is like an automatic program that operates when one establishes connection with it by faith, its inner working mechanism leads automatically with certitude to rebirth upon one's demise in this world.

## 2.5 Profound Faith and Profound Mind

Now, let's focus on the three aspects of the motivation in the highest grade of the nine grades of rebirth: the mind of utmost sincerity, profound mind, and the mind of dedication and aspiration. The method to fulfill the conditions of 1st grade is to combine the three minds with one of the three practices or three blessings: the practice of compassion and non-killing, observing all precepts, or reciting Mahayana sutras. Achieving the highest grade is not easy, and the most challenging among the three minds is the mind of utmost sincerity. As Master Shandao explains, it requires being "genuinely sincere in seeking one's own liberation and genuinely sincere in seeking others' liberation," which already includes the practice of single-mindedly reciting the Buddha's name. However, the so-called profound mind and mind of dedication are easier to attain and actually encompass all nine grades. Those who simultaneously possesses profound faith and the mind of utmost sincerity are rare, and thus they belong to the highest grade in the highest level.

The reason for saying that the profound mind encompasses all nine grades is that Master Shandao dedicates the most writing in his explanations of the concept of liberation through encounters in the profound mind section. We have already explained the idea of liberation by encounters. Now we look at how Master Shandao explains the profound mind:

*"The term 'profound mind' is also synonymous with 'profound faith.' There are two aspects to it: First, it is a firm belief that one is currently an ordinary person trapped in the cycle of birth and death due to past karmic consequences, continuously transmigrating for countless kalpas without any opportunity for liberation. Second, it is a firm belief that, relying on the fulfilled forty-eight vows of Amitabha Buddha, one can be embraced in the Pure land without doubt or hesitation, and that by relying on His vow power, one can attain rebirth. Moreover, it*

*is a firm belief that Shakyamuni Buddha expounded the practice of observing this contemplation sutra's Three Meritorious Deeds and the nine grades of rebirth, certifying and praising that those who count on him will surely be born there. Also, it is a firm belief that in the Amitabha Sutra, countless Buddhas of infinite worlds praised and encouraged the ordinary people who believe the fulfilled vow of Amitabha and confirmed their births there."*

The profound mind, or profound faith, is essentially divided into two aspects: faith on oneself and faith on Amitabha. Faith on oneself means acknowledging one's current state as an ordinary person in the Dharma-ending age, constantly revolving within the cycle of birth and death, unable to attain liberation through one's own efforts. Faith in Amitabha Buddha is the belief that His vow power is absolutely true and real, capable of saving ordinary beings like oneself. These two aspects of profound faith, like the two sides of a single leaf, are inseparable. Because of faith on the powerlessness of oneself in obtaining liberation, one wholeheartedly relies on Buddha Amitabha; and because of one's faith in the Buddha's vow power, one's own status as an ordinary being is not an obstacle to liberation but a stepping stone to rebirth.

If one believes they can achieve Arhatship or become a Bodhisattva in this life, there would be no need to believe in the Pure land. However, because we believe we are humble ordinary person in the Dharma-ending age, we wholeheartedly entrust ourselves to the Pure land of Amitabha Buddha. This implication is present in all nine grades, from the highest grade in the first class to the lowest grade in the lowest class. Followers of the 5th grade, for instance, obviously do not believe they can attain Arhatship in this life. Similarly, evil beings in the lowest grade, at the sight of hellfire upon death, instantly believe they are ordinary beings trapped in the cycle of karma.

It is important to note that the object of profound faith is not the doctrines or theories of Mahayana or Theravada but the belief that one is an ordinary being trapped in the cycle of birth and death and that Amitabha Buddha will save ordinary beings. The mind of dedication and aspiration is a natural extension of profound faith, meaning dedicating or transferring one's merits and virtues to be born in the Pure land. If we say that profound faith and the mind of dedication and aspiration determine whether one can be reborn, then readers may wonder about the "practice" aspect, as Pure land Buddhism emphasizes the Threefold Practice of Faith, Vows, and Practice. What does "practice" mean in the context of the nine grades of rebirth?

Master Shandao provides an explanation in his annotations:

*"Question: What is the difference in the meaning of 'vows' and 'practice'?*

*Answer: As mentioned in the sutra, 'Practice alone is empty and ineffective; vows alone are void and powerless. Only when vows and practice complement each other can they be effective.' Therefore, in this treatise, it explicitly states that making vows does not require any particular practice. Thus, without immediate attainment of rebirth, making vows become the causes for future rebirths and not the immediate cause for immediate rebirth after it. The question may arise, 'Why are they said to not be born?' The answer is that upon hearing the teaching of the Western Pure land's incomparable bliss, they immediately make the vow, 'I also wish to be born there.' Once this statement is made, their life does not continue further; hence, it is called a 'vow.' In the contemplation sutra, ten recitations of the Buddha's name include ten vows and ten practices. What does it mean to fulfill them? Saying 'Namo' is taking refuge and making vows and dedications. Saying 'Amitabha Buddha' is the practice. With this significance, rebirth is certain."*

Therefore, with profound faith and dedication, repeating Namo Amitabha ten times fulfills all the necessary practices. There is such a singularity in the Pure land Buddhism that making vow and practice it are inseparable and combined in one instance. In the recitation "Namo Amitabha," "Namo" encompasses vows, dedications, taking refuge, and profound faith, while repeating "Amitabha Buddha" or Amitabha inherently carries the merits of practice. Hence, reciting Buddha Amitabha's name ten times satisfies all conditions for rebirth.

## 2.6 One-Day Fasting and Precepts observance Practice for 5th grade

Of course, when we look for corresponding texts in the scriptures using Master Shandao's explanations, we find that "rebirth in ten recitations" appears in the lowest grade and birth. "Ten recitations of Amitabha's name" means that after completing ten recitations, there will be "no further continuation of this life." This seems to suggest that "rebirth in ten recitations" must take effect only at the moment of death, and at other times, one cannot rely solely on ten recitations of Amitabha's name to determine rebirth. There is a clear answer to this question, which we will address when dealing with the issue of the moment of death. For now, we do not need to dwell on this. "Rebirth in ten recitations" applies to the lowest grade for evil people to be reborn; this is clearly not the typical situation for believers in Pure land. In reality, anyone who recites Mahayana scriptures and firmly believes in their own rebirth can achieve grades higher than the 9th grade.

However, profound faith itself is intangible. If a believer's confidence in their rebirth grade is not firm enough, fortunately, the practice in one grade provides something very tangible and practical, enough to dispel all doubts about rebirth and one's rebirth grade. The practice in that grade is effortless compared to all other practices, and it provides a sense of practical certainty and ritualistic experience. By combining faith in the Pure land with dedication and that practice, one determines their rebirth. This is the practice of the 5th grade: "If there are sentient beings who uphold the eight precepts or the novice precepts for one day and night, and dedicate the merit to seek rebirth in the Land of Ultimate Bliss while using incense to worship Amitabha. When such a practitioner is approaching the end of their life, they will see Amitabha Buddha and his retinue emit golden light while holding seven jeweled lotus flowers, which they offer to the practitioner. The practitioner will then hear a voice from the sky, praising, "Good wo/man, due to your virtuous deeds and your accord with the teachings of all Buddhas of the past, present, and future, I have come to receive you." The practitioner will then see oneself seated on the lotus flower, which immediately closes, and they will be reborn in the Western Pure land. "

This practice involves upholding the Eight Precepts for a continuous twenty-four hours or observing the novice precepts and dedicating the merit for rebirth. This practice is quite easy to achieve. At our Cundi Dharma institute, we have conducted annual Eight Precepts retreats, where participants observe silence, eat lightly or take vegetarian meals for twenty-four hours in independent temples or monastic settings. Apart from this, they recite the Buddha's name, Mahayana scriptures, perform circumambulations, recite mantras, and at the end, dedicate the merit for rebirth in the Land of Ultimate Bliss during 24 hours. Observing the precepts for twenty-four hours is more accessible and provides a sense of assurance for modern laypeople than the practices in other grades. With inserting oneself in the collective practice, the environment is more immersive and precepts easier to observe than in solitude.

For those in the 4th grade, they are required to "observe the Five Precepts, uphold the Eight Precepts for rebirth, and cultivate the various precepts." The duration of upholding the precepts is not specified, and it should be understood as a lifetime commitment, which is very challenging to maintain for ordinary people. Hence, the practice of upholding the Eight Precepts for one day and night in the 5th grade is a suitable practice of rebirth for modern lay practitioners. After completing the practice of dedicating the merit for rebirth through twenty-four hours of upholding the precepts, one no longer needs to worry about rebirth because rebirth at the end of this life is certain, as explicitly stated in the Contemplation Sutra.

In conclusion, from the perspective of actual practice, regardless of which grade within the nine grades is suitable for oneself, we need profound faith, which means having profound faith in oneself as an ordinary being and profound faith in Amitabha Buddha's salvation of ordinary beings. In terms of practice, one can adopt any of the practices specified in the first six grades. Based on our experience, considering the current situation of lay practitioners, the specific practice of upholding the Eight Precepts for one day and night, as stipulated in the 5th grade, greatly enhances the profound faith of lay practitioners. This profound faith itself activates Amitabha Buddha's vow power and becomes a fitting, tangible practice.

## 2.7   Bodhicitta

As lay Buddhists, apart from the more challenging practices of the 1st grade, 4th grade, and the relatively easy practice of 5th grade, the practices of the 2nd grade birth and 3rd grade in the first five grades are also accessible for lay Buddhists.

For the 2nd grade, "it is not necessary to recite, or memorize various Mahayana scriptures, but to have a good understanding of the meanings and implications of its teachings, not being disturbed by the profound meaning of the first truth, and having profound faith in the cause and effect without defaming Mahayana. By dedicating the merit from this practice, one seeks rebirth in the Land of Ultimate Bliss." In practical terms, this means reading Mahayana sutras at times and think or visualizing the scenes described in the sutra. For example, reading the *Avatamsaka Sutra* and visualizing the scenes depicted in the text, or think the principles presented in the Lotus Sutra. As long as we regard the teachings presented in the Mahayana sutras as the truth conveyed by its words, then it becomes a good understanding of the meanings and implications of it. Such an understanding of Mahayana sutras already holds great merit, and by dedicating this merit for rebirth in the Land of Ultimate Bliss, one can attain the the 2nd grade.

The *Contemplation Sutra* does not specify the frequency required for this practice, and Master Shandao explains that a constant recitation of sutras every day is not necessary here to avoid overlapping with the reading and reciting of Mahayana sutras in the 1st grade. Therefore, lay practitioners can dedicate this merit to rebirth in the Pure land by reading sometimes Mahayana scriptures, which will lead to attaining the grade of the high class middle level birth.

As for the 3rd grade, it also involves having profound faith in the law of cause and effect without defaming Mahayana. However, in this case, there is an intermittent faith in cause and effect, sometimes the individual believes it and sometimes not, hence it is termed "intermittent faith." In our actual experience, many lay practitioners frequently believe in cause and effect when it aligns with their interests but stop the belief when it conflicts with one's own interest. "Intermittent faith" describes this attitude, but such an attitude does not conflict with rebirth. Regarding the understanding of the Mahayana doctrine, i.e., the truth of interdependent origination and emptiness, ordinary beings in the 3rd grade may not grasp or comprehend it like those in the 2nd grade, but they do not reject or slander the Mahayana emptiness teachings. This attitude is accessible for lay Buddhists. In terms of practice, they also need to generate the mind of supreme Bodhicitta, the aspiration to attain Buddhahood and then return to the cycle of birth and death to deliver sentient beings universally. By generating this single thought and dedicating it for rebirth in the Land of Ultimate Bliss, one can attain the 3rd grade. Given that we believe in Buddhist causality and the teachings of the 'Contemplation Sutra', although it becomes certain that we ourselves will certainly attain rebirth in the Pure land, we aspire also to save our non-believing parents, our beloved ones, and friends, and this motivation is also Mahayana aspiration, it is Bodhicitta. We vow to become Bodhisattvas who will not regress in their progress after attaining rebirth in the Pure land, and then return to cycle of three realms to save our once loved ones. This aspiration is also a kind of supreme Bodhicitta and will lead to rebirth in the 3rd grade in the Pure land.

By relying on Buddhist causality and study of the Contemplation Sutra, it becomes clear that achieving 2nd or 3rd or 5th grade is easy for lay Buddhists. Rebirth is not a difficult matter, and its certainty is clearly set forth in the Contemplation Sutra. Lay practitioners no longer need to laboriously and anxiously recite the Buddha Amitabha's name every day to pray for the certainty of rebirth, nor do they need to think that their worldly affairs and occupations obstruct their rebirth. *They can trust that dedicating the merit from their recitation of sutras or one-day fasting will lead to rebirth with absolute certitude.* This liberates lay practitioner's anxiety of their inevitable attachment to worldly matters, there is no conflict between their worldly occupation and their transcendent liberation.

As stated earlier, after dedicating the merit of upholding

the Eight Precepts and reciting the Buddha's name for rebirth in the Pure land, we will not only attain rebirth, but at least we will attain the 5th grade. After upholding the precepts, reciting the Buddha's name is still possible, but it is no longer a practice as a means for the purpose of rebirth. It becomes a means to eliminate countless past and present karmic obstructions of sentient beings in our circumstances, to allow more beings to hear the Buddha's name, and to create the karmic conditions for the rebirth of other sentient beings, as well as to express gratitude for Amitabha Buddha's boundless compassion.

*Since rebirth and liberation are certain at the moment of death, our worldly work and interactions with others are no longer obstacles to liberation but become a kind of nourishment, a practice of Bodhisattva conduct.* Knowing that rebirth is certain, we can now attribute different meanings to our worldly activities. Our professions and jobs are not merely means of earning a living; they inherently possess inner value in contributing to society and others. Our careers themselves hold worldly merits and virtues. Most importantly, your success in your profession can become an opportunity to introduce Buddhism to others.

As practitioners of our Cundi dharma, Amitabha Buddha solves our issues after death, while Cundi Bodhisattva takes care of our current worldly issues. Amitabha Buddha fulfills our wish for liberation after exhausting our karmic body, and Cundi Bodhisattva fulfills our present secular wishes. The dedications in our daily Cundi incantation practice encompass all achievements in all specific, the most concrete worldly matters, from job offer to happy relationship. Therefore, our achievements in our secular life are manifestations of Cundi Bodhisattva's virtues, powers and merits. Even the happiness and harmony of your family, and the fulfillment of all your aspirations, are the embodiment of Cundi Bodhisattva virtues. If these achievements receive admiration from your colleagues and friends, you can tell them about your understanding of Cundi Bodhisattva and Buddhism. Even if they do not believe or understand, you are planting the seeds of great virtues in them. Thus, the achievements in our secular life become a form of Bodhisattva conduct. Through our efforts, we not only work to achieve success but also create opportunities for Buddhism to flourish in the world and form the foundation for the Mahayana practices of lay practitioners.

Similarly, we can also guide our parents to aspire to be reborn in the Land of Ultimate Bliss based on the nine grades of rebirth. We know that the three lower grades are targeted at evil ordinary beings who develop the aspiration for rebirth in the Land of Ultimate Bliss simply due to hearing immense joys living in it from good spiritual advisors, while seeking liberation from the sufferings of the three evil paths. Most of our parents are not evil beings but ordinary individuals. The requirement for their rebirth should not be higher than those of evil people. They only need to develop the aspiration for rebirth by hearing about the joy of the Land of Ultimate Bliss from a good-knowing advisor and reciting the Buddha's name several times. In the case of our parents, we are the good spiritual advisors. How can we explain the joy of the Land of Ultimate Bliss to them? My mother is a typical Chinese mother who has the greatest fear of not seeing her children after her death. I told her, "Mom, in the Land of Ultimate Bliss, there is a mirror through which you can see your children. After you pass away, you can not only see what we are doing now but also what we did in the past and what we will do in the future." After hearing about this, my mother said, "Is there such a wonderful thing? When I die, I can still see you from a mirror and we will receive in the same place. That's great; I want to go there." Her "wanting to go there" expresses her aspiration, signifying that her motivation fulfills the first requirement of rebirth in Pure land. When we teach her to recite the Buddha's name, and she recites "Namo Amitabha", her practice is complete; it means that Amitabha Buddha confirmed that my mother can be reborn in the Pure land. By doing this, we not only help our parents generate the necessary motivation for rebirth but also embody our Bodhicitta. Our act of guiding our parents to aspire to the Land of Ultimate Bliss is an expression of our Bodhicitta, the altruistic attitude towards others. Thus, we have provided our parents with all necessary and sufficient conditions for rebirth in the Pure land and have elevated our own grade of rebirth through the role of being good spiritual advisors to our parents.

In this way, based on our unwavering confidence in rebirth through the nine grades, our worldly occupation and aspiration to transcendent liberation as Buddhists become harmonious. Even if our worldly achievements do not impress others, they are never obstacles to our transcendent liberation. No one is so busy such that s/he could not uphold the Eight Precepts for twenty-four hours. Our relationship with family members, the harmony and love between us and them, are all opportunities for us to become good spiritual advisors and create conditions for their rebirth in the Pure land. The nine grades of liberation in the Pure land provide us with the assurance of rebirth, and our doings in this world after acquiring the faith in Pure land become Bodhisattva conduct to varying degrees. While we do not claim that we attain the Bodhisattva position of non-retrogression in this life by such faith as the Japanese Jōdo Shinshū states, we believe that after gaining the certainty of rebirth in the Pure land, our actions truly enable Buddhism to be present in the world, laying the foundation for the Mahayana practices of lay practitioners.

Chapter

# 3

Repeating Buddha Name and Single-mindedness

## 3.1  Samadhi and Uninterrupted Single-mindedness

As we know, traditional Chinese Pure land Buddhism does not primarily interpret the standard of rebirth in terms of the nine grades of rebirth. In practice, it often emphasizes the importance of repeating Buddha's name in concentrated, undistracted state of mind, the so-called single-mindedness. The scriptural basis for this emphasis can be found in a passage from the *Amitabha Sutra*, which states as follows:

*"Shariputra, good men or good women upon death will be receivedby Amitabha Buddha and a multitude of holy beings if they hear the name of Amitabha Buddha, uphold his name, and maintain undistracted single mind, for one day, two days, three days, four days, five days, six days, or seven days. At that moment, their minds will not be*

*disturbed, they will be reborn in Amitabha Buddha's Pure land."*

This passage seems to be the only instruction in *Amitabha Sutra* that outlines the way to rebirth attainment. The statement that "good men or good women have good roots, merits, and favorable conditions," naturally leads people to understand that rebirth requires the accumulation of good roots, merits, and causal conditions concerning the Pure land. Within this understanding, one needs to practice repeating the Buddha's name for one to seven days with undistracted focus to accumulate the merits. When approaching the end of life, one will be receivedby Amitabha Buddha and other holy beings who manifest themselves, and if one's mind remains undisturbed at that moment due to the power of their practice or merit, one will be reborn in the Land of Ultimate Bliss.

In this interpretation, achieving the state of repeating with an undistracted mind is crucial for rebirth. However, the true test and validation of the power of this samadhi occur at the moment of death when the mind is not disturbed. Since the experience of death is something we can never encounter during this life, we can never be certain if we can attain an undistracted state of mind at that critical moment. The only certainty is that the cultivation of repeating practice increases the likelihood of rebirth. Ideally, one should be able to enter meditative absorption (Samadhi) through continuous repeating and maintain this state regardless of whatever happens to them. However, this is incredibly challenging to achieve, if not outright impossible for ordinary people without extraordinary gift for meditation.

Possible illness and unconsciousness accompanied by Near-death need to be overcome through mindfulness obtained by one's repeating Amitabha practice. Therefore, the idea of predicting the time of death in meditation till Amitabha Buddha appears has been revered by many believers. Legends have been told in these terms in the history of Chinese Pure land Buddhism. This reverence stems from the belief that samadhi state attainment upon death is extraordinarily difficult, which is akin to a miraculous personal achievement in one's practice. People admire the profound meditative states and achievements of such dedicated and gifted practitioners, showing deep reverence for their meditational state of art.

However, two critical questions arise. Firstly, does an undistracted mind attainment through repeating alone guarantee the accumulation of enough good roots, virtues, and causal connections for rebirth? The scripture only mentions that rebirth is not possible without these factors, but does it mean repeating alone is sufficient for accumulating all the required merits for rebirth? Are other virtuous deeds like bridges, roads constructions, engagement in charitable works, or a vegetarian diet perrequites for rebirth? The question remains, and from the perspective of Buddhist exhortations towards virtue, it seems reasonable to consider additional virtuous practices as conductive to rebirth.

Secondly, when is the exact moment of death? What is the conscious state we experience at that time? What does it mean to have an undistracted mind or a disturbed mind during that critical moment? Is it considered undistracted if one is conscious but experiences delusional or confused thoughts? In such a state, can repeating still be considered undistracted? Is it essential to be in a state of clear consciousness and meditative absorption upon death for it to be qualified as having an undistracted mind? Is the moment of death when consciousness gradually fades away? Or is it when one is in a state of unconsciousness but has not yet stopped breathing? In brain death or cardiac death, which moment should be considered as the moment of death? Is the gradual disappearance of warmth from the body considered the moment of death? In all these different moments, if our clear consciousness has disappeared, what remains is the experience of sub-consciousness or the seventh and eighth consciousness. What does an undistracted mind mean in this state, and when exactly does Amitabha Buddha receive us? What state of mind is considered as undistracted? Clearly, it is difficult to answer the questions.

In extreme cases, if someone could predict the exact time of their death and engage in uninterrupted repeating and meditative absorption for several days or hours before death, till Amitabha Buddha appears. This would be the ideal state for rebirth. To achieve this state, a layperson needs to continuously repeat the Buddha's name, engage in virtuous deeds assiduously, and make repeating and virtuous deeds the core of their life, until they could attain one to seven days of Samadhi in their repeating and have absolute certitude that they could maintain it regardless of their bodily state. Such an understanding places very high demands on lay followers and will lead to perpetual anxiety. According to this understanding, a lay follower, uncertain about rebirth before death, may live in constant anxiety about their afterlife. Furthermore, due to the limitations, ordinary people may not possess the natural talents necessary to achieve Samadhi through repeating. Attainment of meditative absorption not only requires a lot of accumulated practice in this life but also extraordinarily natural aptitude of the person. As a result, many individuals may be barred from rebirth in the Pure land.

In the history of Pure land Buddhism, practitioners gradually recognize that taking single mindedness or un-distracted mind as equivalent to Samadhi sets too high the bar for rebirth. Therefore, they attempted to compromise with reality and created distinctions such as "attainment of samadhi through principles," "attainment of samadhi through practices," and "attainment of samadhi through merits." Some even claimed that the moment of Samadhi is achieved when defilements of evil karma are subdued, aiming to lower the threshold for rebirth. However, such gradations of Samadhi levels do not have substantial scriptural basis, nor does such gradual reading of single-mindedness change any of its substance. Achieving Samadhi to the level of "attainment through merits" or subduing defilements is not easy.

This dilemma places Pure land Buddhism, known as an "easy access" compared to other practices, into a difficult situation, as it becomes entangled in the challenging practice of reaching the level of meditative absorption, though the state of the Samadhi is obtained by Nianfo (Chinese), namely repeating name of Amitabha or being mindful of that Buddha. Nevertheless, the understanding of the above-mentioned scriptural passage from the "Amitabha Sutra" is not the only available reasonable interpretation. In the following, we will explore an alternative interpretation based on various versions of this sutra and other Pure land scriptures, it respects the core teaching of Pure land and scriptural nuances.

## 3.2    Xuanzang and Müller's Interpretation of the Amitabha Sutra

When we compare Xuanzang's translation of the Amitabha Sutra in *Praise Sutra of the Pure land Buddha's Reception of Beings* with the same passage in Kumarajiva's translation, the difference is quite apparent, the latter states:

*"Shariputra, all sentient beings born in that Buddha Land accomplish immeasurable and boundless merits. It is not the case that only those beings with few virtuous roots can be reborn in the Pure land of the Buddha of Immeasurable Life and Ultimate Bliss. If there are virtuous male or female individuals with pure faith who hear of the immeasurable merits of the Buddha of Immeasurable Life and Ultimate Bliss in the Pure land, and upon hearing it, contemplate on it for one day, two days, three days, four*

*days, five days, six days, or seven days without confusion. These virtuous male or female individuals, at the time of their death, will have Amitabha Buddha and his assembly of countless disciples of Hinayana and Bodhisattvas encircling them, bestowing by compassion to the individuals to keep their minds undisturbed. After their lives end and they have left their bodies, they will be reborn in the Pure land of Immeasurable Life and Ultimate Bliss."*

Firstly, we notice that the phrase "It is not the case that only those beings with few virtuous roots" is not isolated but is part of the main sentence: "All sentient beings born in that Buddha Land accomplish immeasurable and boundless merits. It is not the case that only those beings with few virtuous roots can be reborn in the Pure land of the Buddha of Immeasurable Life and Ultimate Bliss." The most natural interpretation of this sentence is that because, beings born in the Pure land will accomplish boundless merits, so that, all beings capable of rebirth in the Pure land cannot be those with few virtuous roots. In other words, it is not necessary for us to accumulate numerous virtuous roots to be reborn in the Pure land; rather, whoever can be reborn there is not among those with few virtuous roots.

This statement does not offer a guide to practice but rather describes the inherent qualities of beings reborn in the Pure land. The correctness of this understanding is crucial, since if we understand it this way, the subsequent passage that describes the undisturbed mind upon hearing about the Pure land can be seen as a proof of their virtuous roots needed for rebirth, and the traditional understanding of needing to engage in additional practices, such as performing good deeds or observing dietary restrictions, would not be accurate. For such a critical question, we need further evidence to support this interpretation.

According to Müller's English translation based on the Sanskrit, the sentence can be rendered as: "*Beings are not born in that Buddha country of the Tathāgata Amitāyus as a reward and result of good works performed in this present life.*" Evidently, Müller's translation goes further than that of Xuanzang, as he provides a more precise explanation that beings are reborn in the Pure land due to their virtuous "roots," not because of their actions in this present life. This interpretation may seem contrary to conventional Buddhist principle, so Müller explains his reasoning for this translation in an attached footnote.

Müller's footnote reads: "*Avaramātraka*. This is the Pāli *oramattako*, 'belonging merely to the present life,' and the intention of the writer seems to be to inculcate the doctrine, that salvation can be obtained by mere repetitions of the name of Amitābha, in direct opposition to the original doctrine of Buddha, that as a man soweth, so he reapeth. Buddha would have taught that the *kusalamūla*, the root or the stock of good works performed in this world (avaramātraka), will bear fruit in the next, while here 'vain repetitions' seem all that is enjoyed. The Chinese translators take a different view of this passage. But from the end of this section, where we read *kulaputrena vā kuladuhitrā vā tatra buddhakṣetre kittaprānidhānam kartavyam*, it seems clear that the locative (*buddhakṣetre*) forms the object of the prānidhāna, the fervent prayer or longing. The *sātpuruṣas* already in the *Buddhakṣetra* would be the innumerable men (*manuṣyās*) and Bodhisattvas mentioned before."

According to Müller's interpretation, the understanding of the sentence "Beings are not born in that Buddha country of the Tathāgata Amitāyus as a reward and result of good works performed in this present life" is within the context of the complete sentence: "Then again all beings,

O Sāriputra, ought to make fervent prayer for that Buddha country. And why? Because they come together there with such excellent men. Beings are not born in that Buddha country of the Tathāgata Amitāyus as a reward and result of good works performed in this present life."

Müller's grammatical analysis implies that beings are reborn not due to their virtuous actions in this present life but because of their fervent prayers for that Buddha Land. This fervent prayer, specifically mentioned in the subsequent passage as contemplating upon the Pure land for one to seven days, can be understood as having the sufficient virtuous roots and conditions for rebirth. Müller argues that the contradiction lies in how these fervent prayers or repetitions alone can lead to rebirth in the Pure land, surpassing the notion of relying solely on virtuous actions in this world, which Buddha taught as "as a man soweth, so he reapeth." Müller's question is: Why does the fervent prayer, i.e., the repetition of Buddha's name, become the cause for rebirth rather than virtuous actions in this present life? This question is later answered by a Sui Dynasty stone tablet version of the Amitabha Sutra, where the conclusion is that repeating the name of Amitabha

Buddha alone leads to rebirth and erases all past negative-evil karma. According to this analysis, those who can be reborn in the Pure land are those who have heard and have firm faith in the Pure land teachings. Thus, to be able to hear and have faith in the Pure land teachings indicates that one possesses great virtuous roots and merits from past lives.

Müller's grammatical commentary suggests that sentient beings' rebirth into the Pure land does not solely rely on the karmic fruits of their virtuous actions in this life but rather on their earnest prayers for birth in that Buddha's realm. Specifically, this heartfelt prayer refers to the practice of reciting the Buddha's name from one to seven days, as mentioned later in this passage. Müller finds a contradiction with the original teachings of Buddha: why does this heartfelt prayer, or the act of reciting the Buddha's name, lead to rebirth in the Pure land instead of relying on virtuous actions in this world? The answer to this question can be found when we examine the Chinese translations in conjunction with the analysis provided by Müller.

| Translator | Text |
|---|---|
| Kumarajiva | Shariputra, all the Pure land beings are Avaivart... Shariputra, the sentient beings who hear of the Pure land of Immeasurable Life and Ultimate Blissshould, should make a vow to be born there. Why? This is the gathering place for good and virtuous people. Shariputra, beings with less good roots, blessings or affinities will not be able to be born there. |
| XuanZang | Shariputra, all sentient beings who hear of the countless merits and splendor of Amitabha Buddha's pure land should make a vow to be born there. Why? If they are born there, they will have company of a whole assembly of countless Buddhas and a multitude of holy beings... Shariputra, beings with less good roots, blessings or affinities will not be able to be born in the Pure land of infinite bliss and immeasurable life. |
| Müller | O Sāriputra, sentient beings ought to make fervent prayer for that Buddha country. Why? Because they come together there with such excellent men. Beings are not born in that Buddha country of the Tathāgata Amitāyus as a reward and result of good deeds performed in this present life. |

Clearly, by comparing the two translations, Müller translates "fervent prayers" as designating "vow to be born in that land," and his translation of the Sanskrit expression suggests that rebirth in the Pure land is not attainable through virtuous actions in this world but by vowing to be born there. Vowing to be born in the Pure land encompasses possessing an abundance of virtuous roots and good karma. Vowing to be reborn in the Pure land, in essence, implicate fervent prayers, which involve reciting the Buddha's name. These two aspects are inseparable, as "Namo Amitabha" represents the act of taking refuge in Amitabha Buddha, the reciting of which is both prayer and vow. The repetition of this name is the practice. The contradiction Müller signals is how these "vain repetitions" (referring to repetitive prayers of *Namo Amitabha*) can lead to much greater merit than virtuous actions in this world, prompting the question of why the Buddha exclusively emphasized that rebirth could not be achieved through virtuous actions in this world. Fortunately, the answer to this question is precisely given in the Sui Dynasty's ancient translation of the *Amitabha Sutra*, as recorded on the *Xiangyang Stone Inscription*. In this version of Kumarajiva's translation, after the single-minded concentration, there are additional twenty-one Chinese characters that are not present in the modern edition of the sutra, which reads, "By upholding the name, by calling the name, all offenses will be eradicated; thus, they are endowed with many roots of good virtue." From this, it becomes evident that by combining these three translations, the meaning conveyed by the Buddha to Sariputra in this discourse is that sentient beings cannot be born in the Pure land without possessing many roots of good virtue and karma, the latter means that the many virtues permitting the rebirth cannot be generated by doing good deeds in this life, but by the vow to take refuge in that Buddha and the repetition of that Buddha name, Namo Amitabha. In other words, Rebirth in the Pure land does not depend on virtuous actions performed in this world but on the vow to be born in the Pure land and the recitation of the Buddha's name. Once one vows to be reborn, uttering the Buddha's name naturally becomes fervent prayer, this leads to rebirth, the vow and the repetition are sufficient conditions for rebirth, while the virtuous deeds performed in this life is not even a necessary conditions for the rebirth. If you are reborn in the Pure land, then you are someone with many virtues and good roots. Therefore, the great and many roots of virtues are not accumulated from zero in this life by some Buddhist practice or the doing of good deeds, but that if you hear the name of Amitabha Buddha, believe in the existence of Pure land, have the desire to be reborn there, such contact and connection with Pure land dharma count you as someone with many roots of virtues. If one does not have great and many roots of virtues, one will not be in contact with Pure land dharma, so the roots of virtues originate from accumulation of past good deeds from past lives, which manifest in this life as contact and connection with Pure land dharma.

These analyses are not mere discussions of superficial textual details but aimed at clarifying the aspect of rebirth in this sutra, which is "without having many roots of good virtue and karma, one cannot be born in the Pure land." Our clarification is based solely on analyzing a few dozen words of text from the *Amitabha Sutra*. According to Müller's translation, the reason that Buddha did not entirely emphasize the positive means of attaining rebirth but demonstrated who cannot be reborn, implicates that rebirth cannot be achieved through virtuous actions in this world in the present life. In contrast, we can say that those who make vows and recite the Buddha's name in this life can be reborn. The statements from the *Amitabha Sutra* and Kumarajiva's translation further support the argument for such a reading. The minute analysis we have done does not aim at a technical, textual, or academic sophistication, but for clarifying a religious problem confronted by the Pure land believers: if we do not observe Buddhist precepts or do not observe them rigorously, and if we are not vegetarian, and have not done any evident virtuous altruistic deeds in this life, but solely aspire for the rebirth and repeats sometimes Amitabha Buddha name, should we be counted as having sufficient good roots and merits? According to our analysis of the sutra, it is found that indeed such individuals possess sufficient merits and good roots for rebirth. The answer for this religious question is entirely positive, without any ambiguity.

From the doctrinal perspective, in the previous chapter, we analyzed the Pure land teachings as the fruit vehicle and examined the conditions for rebirth. Master Shandao's teachings have shed light on why encountering the Pure land teachings constitutes significant good roots and causes and conditions for rebirth. In that chapter, our focus was on the nine grades of rebirth. In this section, we have discussed *Amitabha Sutra* where there's no nine grades of rebirth, because the occasion and audience of the Buddha's discourse in this sutra are not the same as those in *Contemplation Sutra*. However, we can still identify the concept of past-life virtues leading to encounter with Pure land dharma in this life in the *Amitabha Sutra*.

In Xuanzang's *Amitabha Sutra* version, it states:
*"Moreover, Sariputra, in this defiled and evil age of the five defilements, if there are good men or good women who, upon hearing phenomena in the Pure land that are extremely difficult to believe in this world, can generate faith and understanding and receive, uphold, recite, and practice in accordance with the teachings, you should know that these people are exceedingly rare and have had planted immeasurable good roots before countless Buddhas in the past. At the end of their lives, they will be reborn in the Western Pure land."*

This passage directly points out that those who hear and believe and then practice according to Pure land Dhama teachings had planted immeasurable good roots from their services to countless Buddhas in their past lives. Perhaps some may think that this is merely a standard phrase for the end of all Buddhist Sutras and should not be over-interpreted. However, the hearing, believing, and practicing in *Amitabha Sutra* are different from those in other sutras because they are primarily embodied in reciting the name "Namo Amitabha." Thus, those who hear and repeat Amitabha Buddha's name have indeed already planted immeasurable good roots, and reciting the Buddha's name itself manifests immense good roots. If we connect this with Müller's translation, where rebirth is not attained through virtuous deeds in this life, it becomes apparent that the many good roots, merits, and favorable conditions are no other than hearing and repeating the name of Amitabha Buddha in this life. Regardless of one's background, being able to hear and repeat the name of Amitabha Buddha in this life implies the maturity of their good roots. If their good roots have not matured from numerous past lives, they would not have the opportunity to hear the name of Amitabha Buddha in this life. This is in conformity with the *Sutra of Infinite Life Span* .

*Sutra on the Buddha of Infinite Life Span* tells how Pure land of Amitabha Buddha was established. The 18th vow of Amitabha is the principle on which the Pure land is built: *If, when I attain buddhahood, sentient beings in the lands of the ten directions who sincerely and joyfully entrust themselves to me, desire to be born in my land, and think of me even ten times should not be born there, may I not attain perfect enlightenment. Excluded, however, are those who commit the five heinous offenses and abuse the Right*

*Dharma.* In the sutra, our Buddha Sakyamuni resumed the spirit of all 48 vows of Amitabha Buddha as: *By the power of that buddha's Original Vows, All who hear his Name and desire birth Will, without exception, be born in his land and effortlessly enter the stage of non-retrogression.*

Fa-xian, in his translation of the Sutra, said: *"When I attain buddhahood, my Name will be Buddha of infinite life, all sentient beings who hear my name, will come to my Pure land."* And *"if sentient beings within the evil realms of hells, hungry ghosts, and animals hear my name, they will give up all sufferings in the three evil realms, be born into my land and practice pure conduct."* Undoubtedly Amitabha Buddha regards his title as the certificate of sentient beings' rebirth into Pure land, and this title contains the power to guide sentient beings who hear and recite it to be born in his Pure land, like a rope pulling them toward it. Regarding the topic we are concerned about, it is worth noting that this verse specifically mentions that sentient beings in the Three Evil Realms will be saved. Beings in the Three Evil Realms cannot perform virtuous deeds because of the inaccessibility of any virtuous actions in their environment. For them, reciting Amitabha Buddha's name is impossible, therefore the only way for attaining liberation is hearing the name of Amitabha Buddha .

Thus, this verifies our interpretation of the Amitabha Sutra, distinguishing those with few meritorious virtues & roots from those with abundant meritorious virtues& roots. The former are those who have not heard or encountered the name of Amitabha Buddha, while the latter refer to those "who hear that Name and desire rebirth", translated by Müller as 'fervent prayers,' the ones who, after hearing about the Pure land, make vows for rebirth, as described in the translation of Xuanzang and Kumārajīva. Therefore, in the distribution section within *Amitabha Sutra*, believers of Pure land are referred to as those whose meritorious virtues have been accumulated with immeasurable Buddhas. From Müller's translation, it is evident that those with abundant meritorious virtues, blessings, and causal conditions are individuals in this world who have heard the name of Amitabha Buddha.

Regardless of realms they belong to, sentient beings who hear the name of Amitabha Buddha, testify their maturity in meritorious virtues from countless kalpas, without which, single hearing of the name of Amitabha Buddha is impossible for them. The same principle applies to the rebirth of evil beings in the *Contemplation Sutra*. Therefore, even in the context of primitive Buddhist doctrine, as stated by Müller, though it may seem contradictory, we must acknowledge that rebirth in the Pure land does not rely on virtuous deeds in this world, but on hearing and reciting the name Amitabha Buddha and making vows for rebirth. This is how beings achieve rebirth.

In other words, the accumulated practice and good karma from past lives enable us to encounter the Pure land teachings in this world. Upon the encounter, the wish to be reborn and reciting the Buddha's name lead us to rebirth. Therefore, such individuals possess tremendous blessings, meritorious virtues, and good roots. If the opportunity to encounter the Pure land in this world relies on each person's good karma from past life, then the immense merits resulting in rebirth through encountering the Pure land teachings in this world in this life are, in reality, bestowed by Amitabha Buddha. Taking refuge in Amitabha Buddha and reciting 'Namo Amitabha' have immeasurable merits. This is clearly due to the connection established between Amitabha Buddha in the Pure land and us in this world through the Buddha's name. The merits we rely on for rebirth ultimately originate from Amitabha Buddha, not from ourselves.

# 3.3 Meaning of "mindful of…"

Above, we have explained the scriptural interpretation of the first essential element for rebirth in the *Amitabha Sutra*, which is the significance of attaining birth in the Pure land through sufficient merits, virtuous roots, and favorable conditions. With the clarification of its meaning, the connection between the other two elements for rebirth–single-mindedness in reciting Amitabha for one to seven days becomes clearer. Xuanzang's translation also demonstrates that "single-mindedness without disturbance" does not refer to the meditative absorption of reciting the Buddha's name or achieving Samadhi. "If there are virtuous men or women with pure faith, upon hearing of the immeasurable virtues and glorious qualities of Amitabha Buddha, the immeasurable, boundless, inconceivable merits, and the majestic qualities of the Pure land of Ultimate Bliss, and upon contemplating it, even if it's for one, two, three, four, five, six, or seven days and nights, their mindfulness will remain steadfast. When these virtuous men or women approach the end of life, Amitabha Buddha together with his countless Hinayana disciples and Bodhisattvas will come to their presence, surround them and bestow compassionate support to keep their minds undisturbed. After abandoning their lives and following the assembly of the Buddha, they will be born in the Pure land of Ultimate Bliss. "

First, it is noteworthy that "mindfulness" is translated as "keeping thinking of something without being distracted" while "the unperturbed mind" is related to an effect created by presence of Amitabha Buddha and his holy assembly before the person on deathbed, so their compassionate support keeps the person unperturbed. The term "mindfulness" is almost synonymous with"unperturbed", with the latter purely counting on the Power of Amitabha Buddha. This is close to meditative absorption, but it is not a result of the practitioner's cultivation, but the power of Amitabha Buddha & His assembly. Now the key point is how to understand the meaning of an ordinary lay practitioner practicing "contemplation" for one to seven days. There is a precondition here, "If there are virtuous men or women with pure faith..." who, upon hearing of the immeasurable virtues of Amitabha Buddha and the glorious qualities of the Pure land, contemplate it; thus, the object of the contemplation or mindfulness is derived from hearing of Amitabha Buddha's virtues and the splendor of the Pure land. "Contemplate" here means intention, just as "Right Intention" in the Noble Eightfold Path refers to correct intention, also translated as "Right Aspiration." Therefore, hearing of the immeasurable virtues and excellent qualities of Amitabha Buddha and yearning for them is contemplation. The key point in "contemplation" lies in "con-", which means taking together in latin, but the Chinese character "xi"( pronounced in Chinese pronunciation system) means taking together something by attaching, tying one thing to another, just as a rope tying a person to an object. What is the object to be tied in this case? Pay attention to "Upon hearing of the immeasurable virtues of Amitabha Buddha and the glorious qualities of the Pure land..." The object is the Buddha's name (the Pure land). According to the *Infinite Life Sutra*, the name of Amitabha Buddha (for His original vow) contains immeasurable merits, and manifests the merits and splendor of the Pure land, signifying the inconceivable virtues of Amitabha Buddha. Thus, in "contemplating it", where the *it* designate qualities of Pure land that shines from the Amitabha's name, the practitioner is bound towards the direction of the Pure land through the name. The crucial aspect of "xi nian" lies in "binding"; just like a rope tying and binding the practitioner to Pure land, and this binding is reliant on the name. It is through repeating the Buddha's name that contemplation of Pure land becomes easier, as it acts like a directional rope guiding, strengthening, and binding our intentions and contemplation towards the object, the Pure land. During repeating, the consciousness can focus on the name of Amitabha Buddha itself, as it already includes the direction towards the immeasurable virtues of the Pure land. Also, people can think of the various goodness of the Pure land and the supreme virtues of Amitabha Buddha. Thus, "hearing and contemplating" in the *Amitabha Sutra* are principles extending from the practice of "desiring rebirth and coming to the Pure land from hearing the name." The "contemplation" and "binding" in "xi nian" describe a form of longing in the desire for rebirth. Thus, binding without being distracted (

"xi nian bu luan") implies that the primary direction of consciousness is toward the Pure land and it is undistracted and unwavering due to the power in the name of Amitabha that the person repeats. As stated before, contemplation refers to intention-one's predominant thoughts are not targeted at desiring to be reborn in this mundane world for another lifetime, or to become a heavenly being, or to be born into a wealthy family, or to be born outside Amitabha's Pure land, but only in the Pure land. Despite the spontaneous emergence of unrelated thoughts from our non-samadhi mind, as long as the primary direction remains unchanged, the direction of consciousness will not be affected, and thus our mind remains unwavering and undistracted. This is what we name single-mindedness. For example, when an academician spends several days, months, or even years in writing a book, disregarding of countless un-related thoughts that cross over his mind during writing process, he is always dealing with the same subject. Then is the academician's mind is in the state of "xi nian", as the predominant direction of her mind is directed towards that subject. Although many other unrelated thoughts may arise during the writing process, they do not deviate the person from the primary subject. He always cares about the subject at hand before completing it, so his mind remains unwavering. Similarly, when we wait for a court judgment, or the list of awarded bonuses which may or may not include our name, or the admission list of a school we are applying for, during this waiting period, we continuously think about the outcome, which will have a significant impact on our life and development. Our thoughts of expectation throughout this period are a form of "xi nian" as we keep longing for the outcome. This longing has a "desire" component, as the motivation to keep repeating Amitabha is the continual desire for rebirth, justly expressed by Namo in Namo Amitabha. This is the essence of "single-mindedness." If we interpret "single mindedness" as a certain form of Samadhi, accomplishment of meditation practice, then for the vast majority of people who cannot achieve this state of mind, where there's zero unrelated thoughts or distraction in the mind of believer for several days, it would lead the believer to constant worries about the state of their mind while they repeat Buddha name and regrets about previous thoughts that deviated from reciting the Buddha's name. Then these worries and regrets would become the main objects of their consciousness, the object of mind would not be the Buddha's name or many virtues of Pure land; instead, the believer would be contemplating their own afflictions, regrets and worries. "Nian" in Buddhism does not solely mean verbal recitation; it encompasses the mind's remembrance, intention, desire, think, and other mental acts. In English translations the reciting in "reciting the Buddha's name" is translated as "keep it in mind," which is closer to the meaning of "reciting" in our everyday language, like "longing for" or "cherishing", and closer to the spirit of the scripture. The rebirth in the Amitabha Sutra is achieved through continuously recite the Buddha's name for one to seven days, always cherishing Amitabha Buddha, thinking Amitabha Buddha, and imagine the wondrous qualities of Pure land of Ultimate Bliss. Continuously reminded by the Buddha's name, the boundless merits of the Buddha's name sustain our "mindfullness", neutralize the effects of inevitable deviation of mind, and enable the rebirth in higher grades for us in the Pure land. Just as when we are sunbathing at beach and our friends pass by and we have to chat with them, our talk does not affect the fact that we are still sunbathing. Regardless of how many random chats we have during sunbathing, our skin color will still deepen, it will be tanned, just as the scattered unrelated thoughts that arise spontaneously during our reciting the Buddha's name do not affect the effectiveness of the practice. The relationship between reciting the Buddha's name and the scattered, distracted, unrelated thoughts during recitation is like our situation in subway. When we board on train of the subway, we know it will take us to our destination. While inside the train, we talk to friends, read books, or do other things, all those activities do not affect the fact that we are continuously moving towards our destination on the metro. The train is in motion, carrying us, and we do not need to run frantically inside the train, trying to run from the back of the train to the front to get closer to the destination. When we recite the Buddha's name, we are bound to Amitabha Buddha, Amitabha Buddha binds us through his name, guiding us, carrying us, and naturally leading us to the Pure land. During this time, our consciousness is not in a state of meditative absorption, and there may be scattered thoughts, dullness, numbness of mind, but it does not affect the power of our thinking on Amitabha, the single-mindedness is maintained by the power of Amitabha through its name recited by us.

## 3.4 Compassionate Blessings that enable the Mind Unperturbed

In the previous sections, we have already explained the concept of "single-mindedness." Now we examine the traditional interpretation of the last rebirth element, "the mind undisturbed" at the time of death. As indicated clearly in Xuanzang's translation earlier, "single-mindedness" and "the mind undisturbed" should be understood together in "if-then" logic: "If there are good men or good women with pure faith who hear the immeasurable Buddha Amitabha's inconceivable merits and virtues and the name of the Pure land, contemplate upon them, and for one, two, three, four, five, six, or seven days and nights, remain steadfast in mindfulness, then, at the end of life, the Buddha Amitabha and all the great assembly of sound-hearers and Bodhisattvas will appear before them. *Endowed with compassionate blessings, they will keep their minds unperturbed.* Having relinquished this life and joined the assembly of the Buddha, they will be born in the Pure land of immeasurable life and ultimate bliss."

In other words, if an ordinary person can achieve what we have previously described as "hearing it, think about it, and care about it ("xi nian")" , then, at the time of death, Amitabha Buddha and other holy beings will manifest before this person. By the power of these holy beings, the person's mind will not be perturbed, and they will be reborn in the Pure land. Neither the practitioner's meditation skills nor the conscious control determines the unperturbed state of mind upon one's death, the distant cause of which is the practitioner's aspiration for the Pure land in their lifetime while the direct cause is the presence of Amitabha Buddha & His holy assembly. In other words, the unperturbed mind is entirely determined by the Other Power (the power of the Buddhas and Bodhisattvas), rather than the Self-power of the believer. Other-power upon one's death presupposes one's previous engagement in hearing, thinking, and aspiring for the Pure land & Amitabha Buddha in one to seven days, repeating Namo Amitabha with single-mindedness. Therefore, the unperturbed mind upon death is not the actual cause of rebirth but rather a description of the state of mind of the believer before rebirth.

In comparison with the traditional interpretation based on Kumarajiva's translation, we can understand why it seems in popular belief that the unperturbed mind must be something achieved by the practitioner after "single-mindedness". Kumarajiva's translation appears to suggest that the practitioner must personally control their mind at the time of Amitabha Buddha's manifestation. On the other hand, Xuanzang's translation makes it clear that the two are not in the relation of coordination but are causally related. As Amitabha Buddha and the holy assembly appear, they bestow their compassionate blessings on the practitioner, resulting in the person's unperturbed mind. Moreover, in Kumarajiva's translation, the phrase ("ji de" in Chinese pronunciation system) can easily be misunderstood as "if" rather than "immediately." Xuanzang's translation clarifies this point: "When the virtuous men come to the end of their lives, the Buddha of infinite life...comes before them. With compassionate blessings, they keep their minds unperturbed. Having relinquished this life and joined the assembly of the Buddha, they will be born in the Pure land of infinite life and ultimate bliss." In other words, when the person's life is ending, Amitabha Buddha and others will appear, bestow their blessings on this person, and the person will immediately be reborn in the Pure land. The unperturbed mind at the time of death and rebirth are connected by time, not by conditions. The unperturbed mind is not the result of the practitioner's doings but the manifestation of the holy beings' power, with the latter being in turn the practitioner's previous one-to-seven days of hearing and constant aspiration for the Buddha's name and the Pure land. If Pure land believers practice according to the *Amitabha Sutra*, they do not need to worry about whether they can achieve the state of unperturbed mind at the time of death, because such a state will naturally come. The Tibetan and English translation of the sutra is more precise in this respect: "Śāriputra, if those sons and daughters of good family hear the name of the Bhagavān Tathāgata Amitāyus and keep it in mind unwaveringly for one, two, three, four, five, six, or seven nights, when the hour of their death arrives, they will depart in an undeluded state. (1.11 *The Display of the Pure land of Sukhāvatī*, 2011).

So far, the passages in the *Amitabha Sutra* that, if in the traditional interpretation, are most likely to cause anxiety among practitioners, have now been elucidated. Essentially, the entire passage clarifies and extends the power of original vows of Amitabha Buddha: "*By the power of that buddha's Original Vows, All who hear his Name and aspire for birth, Will, without exception, be born in his land And effortlessly enter the stage of non-retrogression.*" The essential meaning is that to be born in the Pure land, one needs to have many virtuous roots and merits, which is no other than hearing the name of Amitabha Buddha. Hearing the name of Amitabha Buddha signifies having many virtuous roots and merits. "Single-mindedness without disturbance" refers to the practitioners' hearing, thinking, and single-mindedly repeating the ultimate goodness of the Pure land & Amitabha Buddha for one to seven days before they are received by Amitabha Buddha & the holy assembly and guided to a peaceful rebirth upon death.

Therefore, whether we follow the Nine Grades of *Contemplation Sutra* or the *Amitabha Sutra*, rebirth is not a difficult matter. Those who have heard the Buddha's name already possess great virtuous roots. With this foundation, all that is needed is the aspiration for rebirth to attain the certainty of rebirth. Thus, we have provided our interpretation of the key passage in the *Amitabha Sutra* concerning the practice for rebirth.

## 3.5 *Contemplation Sutra* and *Amitabha Sutra*

In the discussions above, we mainly focused on the *Amitabha Sutra* itself, although we also related *Infinite Life Sutra* closely connected with it (*Amitabha Sutra*, also known as the *Shorter Infinite life Sutra*). The central position of the *Contemplation Sutra* in Master Shandao's teachings being considered, how should we view the relationship between the *Contemplation Sutra* and the *Amitabha Sutra*?

Let us turn to quotation from the *Fourfold Adornment Commentary*: "the Buddha expounded scriptures in different contexts, at different times, for different audiences, and different occasions, addressing different needs and benefits." We can see that *The Contemplation Sutra* and

*The Amitabha Sutra*, as two classics dedicated to the Pure land Dharma Approach, differ from one another in that they were spoken in different circumstances. The specifics of these differences include the timing, location, capacity of the audience, and the benefits bestowed. This distinction is evident in the passages that describe the final teaching for the respective sutras. In *the Contemplation Sutra*, it states, "At that time, when the World-Honored One expounded this teaching, Vaidehi and her five hundred attendants heard what the Buddha said...and suddenly comprehended and attained the Non-Arising Patience." In *the Amitabha Sutra*, the final section continues with a dialogue between Shakyamuni Buddha and Shariputra: "Shariputra, you should know that I, in this Evil Age of the Five Defilements, have accomplished the extremely difficult act and attained Anuttara-samyak-sambodhi. For all sentient beings in the world, I expound this extremely difficult-to-believe Dharma, which is exceedingly difficult." *The Contemplation Sutra* is targeted at ordinary people in the Buddha-ending epoch represented by Vaidehi, while in the other sutra the audience include not only human beings, but also heavenly beings and Bodhisattvas, Hinayana disciples of the Buddha. Thus, from both perspectives of responsive teachings and the presentation of benefits, *the Contemplation Sutra* specifically selects Vaidehi, a laywoman without any previous spiritual attainment, as the audience, targeting ordinary people. On the other hand, *the Amitabha Sutra* continuously engages in dialogue with Shariputra, the famous Arhat disciple of the Buddha, who represent ordinary people plus all other beings spiritually higher than ordinary human beings. Consequently, *the Amitabha Sutra* can be considered as primarily spoken for the Great Arhats, namely for the monastics, and secondarily for all sentient beings. Now, *the Contemplation Sutra* teaches the definite practice for both people who can achieve Samadhi by visualization and ordinary people whose mind is often distracted.

Therefore, from the perspective of liberation by encounter of favorable conditions, *the Amitabha Sutra* primarily expounds teachings for the monastics who possess the conditions and spiritual attainments for practice. Although its audience also includes laypersons, ordinary beings, celestial beings, and others, *the Contemplation Sutra* purely addresses laypersons without any prior spiritual attainments. Thus, according to Master Shandao's view, as laypersons, we should consider *the Contemplation Sutra* as the most appropriate and suitable guidance according to our capacities and affinity. This understanding also helps us comprehend why the translation of *the Amitabha Sutra* by Master translator Kumarajiva could lead to a mainstream Chinese interpretation of the need for achieving the Samadhi level of mindfulness of Buddha recitation for rebirth. His translation was more suitable for monastics who regard liberation as their own responsibility. In this sense, the traditional interpretation where they understand the "single-mindedness" as a meditative state has some basis. However, it may not be appropriate for us laypersons with heavy karmic burdens who completely rely on the Other Power (Amida Buddha's power) for liberation. In our previous discussions, we approached *the Amitabha Sutra* from the perspective of *the Contemplation Sutra*, emphasizing an alternative interpretation of *Amitabha Sutra* that also has very solid textual and doctrinal basis. In essence, we consistently believe in and practice different methods of rebirth according to the Nine Grades of Rebirth as suitable for laypersons' practice. However, for laypersons who prefer the *Amitabha Sutra*, we offer another reading which suits laypersons' conditions as well. From the perspective of liberation by encounter, the teachings we found in the *Amitabha Sutra* quite match the popular interpretations of "single-mindedness" as a form of Samadhi, with the only difference that each method caters to people with their respective tendency and conditions.

Here is a table in which the contexts of the two sutras are listed:

| Sutra | *Contemplation Sutra* | *Amitabha Sutra* |
|---|---|---|
| Person requesting the Dharma Way | Vaidehi | Shariputra |
| Representation | Ordinary people | Arhat |
| Beneficiary | Ordinary people in the dharma-ending age full of defilements | All human beings, heavenly beings, Bodhisattva |

Therefore, in practice, we advocate following the method of rebirth as described in the nine grades within the *Contemplation Sutra*. This involves observing the Eight Precepts for one day and night, reciting the Buddha's name during this period, and then dedicating the merits to rebirth. By doing so, regardless of people favoring the *Contemplation Sutra* system or the practice within the

*Amitabha Sutra*, we can clearly achieve rebirth at the moment of death. Of course, if a practitioner prefers to read Mahayana scriptures or other dhāraṇī, they can achieve the same effect by reading those texts they love during the 24hours of observance of eight precepts and then dedicate the merits to rebirth.

For ordinary beings, the *Contemplation Sutra* is more suitable as it accommodates their situations perfectly. Many ordinary people may not receive the criteria of "firm goodness" or "pure faith" as specified in the Amitabha Sutra for being called "good men and good women." Therefore, the minimum requirement for rebirth for ordinary people should be based on the *Contemplation Sutra*. With ten repeats of the Buddha's name, one can achieve rebirth in the lower grade; with one day of precepts observance and dedication, rebirth in the 5th grade is attainable, and by repeating the *Universal Worthy Bodhisattva's conduct and vows*, a résumé of Mahayana principles and principles from *Flower Adornment Sutra*, one can achieve rebirth in the high grade.

The above explanation of the *Amitabha Sutra* has already indicated that practitioners need not be anxious about the level of their Buddha-repeat practice, nor worry about whether they have accumulated enough good deeds in their lifetime. Instead, they only need to practice by continuously thinking about Amitabha Buddha, the Pure land qualities, within the sound of the Buddha's name for a day and night at any point in their life to achieve natural rebirth. If they practise seven days of Buddha-repeat, they will be reborn in higher grade. However, we have not fully addressed the question of what is meant by the moment of death, or the moment of ending this life, which will be dealt with in the next chapter.

Chapter

# 4

## The Moment of Death

In the preceding chapter, we have discussed the three main elements required for rebirth in the *Amitābha Sūtra*: the accumulation of good roots and merits, single-mindedness in minding Amitabha Buddha, and an undisturbed mind. We initially posed the question of what constitutes the moment in the traditional context. In Xuanzang's translated version, it has been mentioned that the undisturbed mind at the moment of death entirely results from Amitābha Buddha's blessings and other holy beings' support, but the question of happenings and the sight of the Buddha's presence at the moment of death is not fully addressed. The reason for particularly addressing this question here is that the certainty of the moment of death and Amitābha Buddha & other holy beings' presence during one's final moments are not limited to the *Amitābha Sūtra*. In *Contemplation Sūtra*, our foundational scripture, each of the nine grades explicitly mentions what phenomena individuals experience as their lives approach their ends before attaining rebirth. It is particularly noteworthy that in the descriptions of the 6th to the 9th grade, which encompass the non-believers and evil people in the middle (low grade) and low categories, "near-death encountering of wise spiritual guides" is mentioned. These individuals, upon hearing the Dharma or reciting the Buddha's name, are reborn due to the merits of Amitābha Buddha's, the Pure land or Mahayana scriptures. This creates the impression that the ability to repeat the Buddha's name at the moment of death or possessing correct knowledge and insight is crucial. Moreover, when combined with the traditional interpretation of the *unperturbed mind* at the moment of death from the *Amitābha Sūtra*, it appears that both the *Contemplation Sūtra* and the *Amitābha Sūtra* emphasize the same idea: that the most essential practice for rebirth lies in reciting the Buddha's name at the moment of death. However, due to the uncertainty of the timing and conscious state at the moment of death, a powerful recitation practice is still necessary to ensure that one can recite the Buddha's name lucidly and call upon Amitābha Buddha and other holy beings, at the moment of death, to attain rebirth. If this understanding is adopted, then everything we have elaborated and developed earlier lacks a theoretical basis in the practice of lay followers. Therefore, the relationship between the moment of death, the state of consciousness at the moment of death, and rebirth requires specific study.

Firstly, we need to note that, based on the *Contemplation Sūtra*, the first five grades do not explicitly mention reciting the Buddha's name at the moment of death. The contents of these grades indicate what motivations and actions practitioners should cultivate for dedicating merits, which will subsequently lead to encountering Amitābha Buddha and his retinue at the moment of death. The mention of reciting Buddhist Dharma and the Buddha's name only begins from the 6th grade of rebirth. Why is this the case? By comparing the distinctions between the nine stages, the first three grades involve individuals with the Mahayana aspiration. The next two grades involve ordinary individuals seeking personal liberation, or people with Hinayana tendencies. The 6th grade involves non-believers who perform worldly virtuous acts, displaying filial piety and compassion. The lowest three grades involve evil ordinary individuals, who have committed various wrongdoings including the five heinous deeds, severe transgressions of monastic precepts, and further wrongdoings. The reason these last four grades involve encountering Buddhist Dharma and the Buddha's name at the moment of death is evidently due to their lack of contact or deliberate defiance of Buddhism in their lifetime. Their characteristics include never having aspired to reach the Pure land before, thus naturally requiring the aspiration for the Pure land at the moment of death. The *Contemplation Sūtra* describes that these four grades involve reciting the Buddha's name at the moment of death and rebirth, precisely because the merits of reciting the Buddha's name are unparalleled. Even if they only learn about the necessity of reciting the Buddha's name at the very last moment, Amitābha Buddha will still hear and save them. In traditional understanding, it is because the merits and force of the thoughts and willpower at the moment of death are exceptionally strong, surpassing the merits of ordinary thoughts and deeds many times over, that the final thought at the moment of death becomes crucial. It even determines the direction of one's rebirth, allowing even evil individuals to attain rebirth through reciting the Buddha's name. Is it really the case?

# 4.1 Theory of Death in Mahayana Buddhism

Firstly, we need to review near-death theories in Buddhism. In the the opening chapter of *the Yogācārabhūmi-śāstra* death classification within Buddhism is mentioned, which fall into three types: "death due to the exhaustion of lifespan," "death due to the exhaustion of merit," and "death due to inappropriate conduct in diet, medication or impure deeds", corresponding to the exhaustion of karmic consequences in this life, lack of necessities for survival, and the body destroyed by accident. Essentially, the death causes are divided into natural death and accidental death. In the *Treatise*, the process of death, according to the commentary of KuiJi, is divided into three stages: "clear-sharp mind," "fertilizing-life mind," and "actual-death mind". "Clear-sharp mind" is the stage where consciousness remains conscious near death, capable of discerning good and bad and making decisions about various matters, which is referred to as gross cognitive manifestation. "Fertilizing-life mind" follows when consciousness becomes vague, the individual loses cognitive abilities, distinctions between good and bad disappear, and the power of the seventh consciousness, which is the pure ego, is exposed. At this point, individuals can only feel the imminent disappearance of the self and a strong manifestation of ego attachment, fertilizing the life of the dying individual, preparing them to be reborn in the next life. Then comes "actual-death mind", where consciousness is completely obscured, only physical actions remain, and the consciousness gradually departs the body, resulting in body temperature decline. Since the second and third stages are the same for all non-saints, the distinction in their future rebirths in the Six Realms becomes evident in the first stage, the "clear-sharp mind" or gross cognitive manifestations stage. In this stage, individuals have two possibilities: to die with a virtuous mind or with a non-virtuous mind:

*"How does one die with a virtuous mind? Just as when one's life is about to end, one remembers or is reminded of*

*the virtuous practices previously engaged in. Due to these causal conditions, virtuous qualities such as faith arises in the mind, extending even to gross cognitive activities. When subtle cognitive activities arise, the virtuous mind is relinquished, and attaches to the non-conceptual mind. The reason being, at that time, one is unable to recall or reminded of virtuous practices previously engaged in."*

*"How does one die with a non-virtuous mind? Just as when one's life is about to end, one recalls or is reminded of the unwholesome practices previously engaged in. At that time, the unwholesome qualities of greed, hatred, and others arise in the mind, extending to both gross and subtle conceptual thinking. As previously explained, when one dies with a virtuous mind, it is peaceful and tranquil, but when one dies with a non-virtuous mind, it is filled with suffering. When one dies with a virtuous mind, one sees clear and orderly forms, while when one dies with a non-virtuous mind, one sees chaotic forms."*

In other words, when individuals remember virtuous actions or teachings at the moment of death, either through their own recollection or with the help of others, they die peacefully with a virtuous state of mind. If they remember unwholesome actions or teachings, they die in great suffering. There is also a third state at the stage of clear-sharp mind, where death occurs with a unrecordable (avyākhyāta) state of mind:

*"How does one die with a non-remembrance state of mind? This refers to those who have engaged in virtuous or non-virtuous actions, or neither. As their lives come to an end, they cannot remember by themselves, nor are they made to remember by others any of the afore-mentioned actions. At that time, it is neither in virtuous nor non-virtuous state of mind that one dies. It is not a death of peace and tranquility, nor one of suffering and distress. For those who have mostly practiced one kind of action, they may remember that action due to the strength of their previous conditioning. If they have practiced both equally, they may remember either by themselves or through the prompting of others, and they relinquish the remaining mind. At that time, due to the power of these two causes, they die."*

In essence, dying with a non-conceptual mind means

individuals cannot actively recall virtuous or non-virtuous actions. The strongest karmic action from their lifetime automatically surfaces. In this sense, dying with a non-conceptual mind can also be categorized as dying with either a virtuous or a non-virtuous mind. This is easily understood, as Buddhism, being a religion that operates on the principles of accumulating and balancing merits and demerits, will inevitably interpret any state unrelated to virtues or non-virtues within the context of virtues or non-virtues. It is noteworthy that the *Treatise* mentions that those who die with a non-virtuous mind will witness their severe karmic consequences and experience bodily discomfort. This aligns with the descriptions of the deaths of extremely unenlightened beings in the lower class in the Contemplation Sutra. Whether one dies with a virtuous or non-virtuous mind, it reflects the accumulation of karmic conditioning throughout one's lifetime. Although the initial section of the *Treatise* does not explicitly mention karmic conditioning for dying with a virtuous mind, it does emphasize the significance of karmic conditioning in an accumulate way like a balance sheet in the supplementary passages related to dying with a non-virtuous or non-conceptual mind. This implies that the resultant of karmic forces generated by good and bad actions throughout one's life plays a decisive role in determining the transition to the next life during the dying process. It is important to note that even though dying with a virtuous mind can be influenced by one's conscious intent, the greatest impact lies in a peaceful bodily death. The factors that truly influence the outcome of the next rebirth in the Six Realms are the cumulative results of positive and negative karmic actions:

*"At that time, due to the power of these two causes, they die, which are additionally conditioned by the play of discourse and the power of virtuous and unvirtuous actions. Having exhausted the consequences of previous life actions in this life, if one has engaged in unvirtuous actions, one will see the first sign of unloved consequence of those evil actions... It should be understood that this is how individuals transition from brightness to darkness. If one has exhausted the suffering of unvirtuous actions from last life in this life and has done virtuous deeds in this life, the karmic consequence will be the contrary to the former case, it should be known that this individual transitions from darkness to brightness at the moment of death." "At the*

*time of death and rebirth, like a balance scale, when one side is low, the other side is high. For the intermediate soul ( 中有 , the soul between the end of this life and rebirth in the next life), it necessarily has sense organs. For those who have committed evil actions, their intermediate soul is like a black sheep or dark night. For those who have performed good actions, their intermediate soul is like white clothing sheen or clear mooned night."*

In summary, when sentient beings in kāmadhātu (realms of desires) approach death and experience gross cognitive state of mind (clear-sharp mind), it is a reflection of the virtuous and non-virtuous minds that they have cultivated and their corresponding attachment and aversion to their karmic outcomes. It is not merely a momentary worldly virtuous thought, at the time of death, that determines whether one will attain a better destination after death, as some may think. In reality, dying with a virtuous thought can lead to a peaceful death, but it cannot change the trajectory of being reborn as an animal if one's accumulated karma throughout their life dictates such an outcome. In principle, whether one dies with a virtuous or non-virtuous thought at the moment of death is not a matter of personal control, but rather a result of one's lifetime actions. It is not the cause for changing or determining the transformation of one's next rebirth. In fact, dying peacefully with a virtuous thought occurs because the individual sees the favorable destination they will reach in their next life. It is only a sign rather than a cause. Conversely, dying in suffering due to a non-virtuous thought is because they foresee the Three Evil Realms. These previews of the conditions for the next life at the time of death result from the cumulative actions of one's lifetime. This understanding is also expressed in the *Avataṃsaka Sūtra* (*Flower Adornment Sutra*):

*"For example, a person about to die sees the consequences of their actions: those who have committed evil actions see all the realms of suffering such as hell, animals, and hungry ghosts. They may see jailers holding weapons, cursing prisoners, or taking them away. They may hear cries and lamentations, or see rivers of ash, boiling pots, knife mountains, sword trees—various forms of torment. Those who have done virtuous actions see heavenly palaces, countless heavenly beings, celestial maidens, and various garments and decorations. Although their body has not died yet, due to the power of their*

*actions, they perceive such phenomena."*

It is even more directly stated in *The Laṅkāvatāra Sūtra*:

"Ānanda, in the cycle of birth and death in the world, birth arises from habits, and death arises from discontinuities. When approaching death, the bodily warmth is not abandoned yet. During that time, the good and the evil of all one›s lifetime are suddenly evident and occur simultaneously; the conformity to habits, which is life, and the reverse of it, the death, are two *habitus that receive each other at the moment of death*."

The folk belief of a "carousel of all events of life" during death transitions in China, and similar beliefs found among many cultures worldwide, actually align with Buddhist theories of life and death. The final stage of an individual's consciousness before death involves summarizing the merits and demerits they have accumulated in life. With this understanding, let us return to the interpretation of death in the *Contemplation Sutra.*

## 4.2 The Process of Approaching Death in the *Contemplation Sūtra*

Firstly, let us observe the legitimate causes for rebirth of three types of individuals within the lower class Rebirth. *"Those born in the 7th grade include sentient beings who commit numerous evil deeds, even though they do not slander the scriptures such as the Pratyutpanna-sūtra. The foolish individuals engage in evil practices without any remorse or regret. When their lives are about to end, they encounter good spiritual advisors and extol the titles of the Twelve Mahayana Scriptures. Hearing various scriptural names, their immensely heavy negative karma accumulated over thousands of eons become eliminated. The wise one then teaches the individual of joined palms and fingers interlocked in repeating 'Namo Amitābha Buddha.' Due to repeating the Buddha's name, they eliminate the karmic obstacles of fifty billion eons of samsara. At that moment, that Buddha sends forth transformational Buddha, Avalokiteśvara, Mahāsthāmaprāpta, who immediately appear before the practitioner and declare, 'Excellent, excellent, virtuous man! Because you repeated the Buddha's name, all your offenses are destroyed. I have come to receive you.' As soon as these words are spoken, the practitioner beholds the transformational Buddha's radiance illuminating the entire room , and upon seeing this, they depart with joy as their life ends."*

It can be seen that the sutra mentions three instances of these individuals' offenses and evil karma being eradicated. Wicked individuals in the Lower Grade Rebirth continuously commit evil deeds without any sense of remorse or repentance, accumulating immensely heavy negative karma throughout their lives. However, at the moment before death, upon hearing the names of Mahayana scriptures, they eliminate the felonious karma of a thousand eons; repeating the Buddha's name purifies immeasurable grave offenses. Approaching death, they immediately experience the fruition of these two acts: the result of hearing the Mahayana scriptures' names and repeating the

Buddha's name. This outcome is Amitābha Buddha coming to guide them. These individuals were initially "foolish," but after performing these two acts, they are transformed into "virtuous men." Amitābha Buddha confirms that they have repeated the Buddha's name and that all offenses have been eliminated. This indicates that rebirth is not solely granted due to reciting the Buddha's name or hearing the names of Mahayana scriptures at the moment of death. Instead, it is the merit generated from repeating the Buddha's name and hearing the names of Mahayana scriptures in their lifetime that facilitates and brings forth rebirth. Their timely engagement in these actions during the final moments simply results in a swift fruition, as the presence of the holy assembly in the Pure land is inherently connected to the moment of death. This prompts the question: Does an individual's habitual recitation of the Buddha's name not absolve them of the karmic consequences of five billion eons of samsara? Is the power of the Buddha's name's purification and karma erasure solely attributed to the practitioner? Isn't the extraordinary merit of the Buddha's name a manifestation of Amitābha Buddha's vow and power? Therefore, we must acknowledge that repeating the Buddha's name possesses the same exceptional merit regardless of the moment of repeating it in an individual's life, as Amitābha Buddha does not discriminate based on one's conscious state. Amitābha Buddha embodies compassion and equality. Amitābha Buddha's vow and power remain constant and fulfilled. Thus, anyone who recites his name accumulates this merit throughout their life, unaltered by the practitioner's conscious state or stage of cultivation.

For sentient beings in the Three Evil Realms, Amitābha Buddha also offers salvation, let alone ordinary human beings. The power of Amitābha Buddha's original vow is definite and already accomplished. As long as one recites his name, merits will undoubtedly be bestowed upon the practitioner's life, unaffected by the practitioner's state of consciousness or level of practice, and its immeasurable virtues remain unchanged. The extremely evil mundane beings of the 8th grade, upon hearing "Amitābha Buddha's ten powers and majestic virtues... his radiant luminous power... the virtues of precepts, concentration, wisdom, and liberation," "all the sins of eighty billion kalpas of births and deaths are eradicated."

Similarly, for the mundane beings of the 9th grade, who have committed the five heinous acts and ten evil deeds, "having fully executed ten recitations of 'Namo Amitābha Buddha,' due to the continuous recitation of the Buddha's name, all the sins of eighty billion kalpas of births and deaths are eradicated." The sutras never affirms that the reason for the purification of sins by reciting the Buddha's name is due to the occurrence of it *at the moment of* death; rather, the sins are eradicated solely due to the recitation of the Buddha's name in general. From this, it can be understood that the process of rebirth for the extremely evil mundane beings of the Lower Three Grades, as described in the Contemplation Sūtra, can be combined with the concept of unrecordable (avyākhyāta) state of mind at the time of death, as discussed in the *Yogācārabhūmi-śāstra*, for a clearer understanding.

*"When individuals with virtuous or non-virtuous nature come to the end of their life, they remember either naturally or influenced by others the good or evil deeds they have done, the one with the most potent karmic tendencies come to the individual's mind, which remains while all others are forgotten."*

Evil-doers within the last three grades of the lower class Rebirth naturally recollect their non-virtuous actions as death approaches. However, due to suddenly encountering Amitābha Buddha's name, the phrase 'Namo Amitābha' becomes the most potent karmic tendency, transforming their consciousness from being steeped in evil karma to repeating the Buddha's name. Notably, the wicked individuals within the three lowest grades have received instructions from good spiritual advisors, indicating that they have reached the phase of viewing sign from balance sheet of karmic consequences and have clearly seen the terrifying destinies awaiting them. Yet, upon encountering the Buddha's name, their trajectory shifts entirely, underscoring the immense power of the Buddha's name. It dismantles the accumulated power of their immensely heavy evil karma, turning their course away from the Three Evil Paths, fully reorienting them towards rebirth in the Pure land. This clarifies the principles of rebirth for evil-doers within the last three grades.

The rebirth principles for individuals in 6th grade are easily understood. These individuals are originally virtuous people of the secular world and may be reborn in superior households in either the human or celestial realms. However, encountering the teachings of the Pure land during their lifetime leads them to rebirth in the Pure land. In summary, the rebirth of individuals in the last four grades among the Nine Grades is not determined solely by their repeat of the Buddha's name upon death, but by the fact that they have repeated the Buddha's name during their lifetime. What counts is not the moment of repeating but the repeat itself. This aids in understanding why repeating the Buddha's name upon death is not mentioned in the first five grades of rebirth in the *Contemplation Sūtra*. These individuals have already repeated the Buddha's name or dedicated immeasurable merits to the Pure land in their lifetime, obviating the need for recitation upon death. Their attainment of rebirth, guided by the holy assembly, is certain, requiring no action or preparation upon death.

In conclusion, an individual's inclination towards a certain realm upon death is determined by their cumulative karmic potential. This karmic potential is the total of karma from all their actions throughout their life. A strong directive force is inherent in such actions as observing the Eight Precepts by repeating the Buddha's name for a day and night or repeating Mahayana sutras, and dedicating the merits to rebirth in the Pure land, the merit of which surpasses the cumulative karmic potential of all other actions, thus ensuring the individual's rebirth. Even if one does other deeds thousands of day and night during their life-time, the merit accumulated during this single day dictates their postmortem trajectory. Similarly, grave karmic potential that characterized the Five Heinous Deeds and Ten Grave Offenses outweighs other actions' karmic potential. However, as elucidated in the *Contemplation Sūtra*, the powerful merits generated by reciting the Buddha's name can neutralize or eliminate the karmic consequences of the Five Heinous Deeds and Ten Grave Offenses. Thus, it becomes evident that rebirth is not solely the result of repeating the Buddha's name *at the moment of* death but of having repeated the Buddha's name and aspired for rebirth in the Pure land during their life-time. This aligns with both the first five grades in the *Contemplation Sūtra* and the *Amitābha Sūtra*.

## 4.3　Certitude of "End-of-this-life" Moment

In fact, neither Buddhist scriptures nor the *Treatise* explicitly state whether the consciousness of deceased person in any type of death will undergo the stage of clear-sharp cognition. The question to consider is whether those die a sudden death will also experience this stage of cognition upon death? In our general understanding, in case of accidental and violent death, clear cognition stage doesn't seem to occur before death or the pre-terminal phase. For example, in instances such as a gunshot to the head or sudden death in a truck accident in the street, from a medical perspective, sudden brain death occurs, in which case, will there still be a "carousel of life-events" displaying the entirety of one's good and evil deeds? Will there be an emergence of thought of virtue or malevolence from habit? This is a challenging question. Judging from

Buddhist texts, individuals will still experience the stage of clear-beneficial cognition, though it is difficult to imagine concerning a clinical human body structure. This question is merely a specific case within the broader topic of determining the moment of approaching death. We have previously demonstrated that due to the merits of repeating the Buddha's name, Amitābha Buddha will guide us during the stage of clear-sharp cognition at the moment of death. Now, the question is, at what exact fraction of a second or hour before death does the stage of clear cognition at the time of approaching death occur? Is this stage of clear-sharp cognition the time when a person is about to lose consciousness or the time before falling into a coma and brain death on the sickbed? Our previous conclusion is that as long as one has ever repeated the Buddha's name with the intention of rebirth and has fulfilled the stipulations of the Amitābha Sūtra, or has practiced any of the first five grades of meditation practice according to the *Contemplation Sūtra*, there will be a Buddha coming to welcoming them upon death, providing compassionate blessings to ensure that the mind remains unperturbed and guiding them to the Pure land. Therefore, let us now explore how to ascertain the exact time when the Buddha comes to receive the person. In fact, the question of the exact moment holds no importance for believers of Pure land.

In the *Infinite Life Sūtra*, the eighth vow of the Bhikṣu Dharmākara states, "If I attained buddhahood, humans and devas in my land were not endowed with the faculty of knowing others' thoughts, or thoughts of billions of sentient beings of a hundred thousand koṭis of nayutas of buddha lands. Then I may not have attained perfect enlightenment." We can call it intelligence of other-minds. The fifth vow states," If I attained buddhahood, humans and devas in my land were not able to recall their former lives, nor do they know at least the events that occurred during the previous hundred thousand koṭis of nayutas of kalpas. Then I may not have attained perfect enlightenment. "This is the "Insight-into-past-lives Vow". The sixth vow is the Divine-Eye Vow. "If attained buddhahood, humans and devas in my land were not to be endowed with divine eye of seeing at least a hundred thousand koṭis of nayutas of buddha lands. I may not have attained perfect enlightenment." Since the Land of Ultimate Bliss is already in existence, it is evident that all beings in the Land of Ultimate Bliss are endowed with capacities of Insight-into-past-lives and penetration-into-others' thoughts. This refers to their perception of countless sentient beings' past actions, behavior, thoughts, and their current thoughts as well. As the future fate is the result of the accumulation of past karma and present intentions, combined with environmental factors, the Divine Eye Insight enables beings in the Ultimate Bliss Land to directly observe events related to the material aspects of the infinite lands. Therefore, beings in the Land of Ultimate Bliss can inherently observe the past and present of countless beings in other worlds and foresee their future. Being the creator of his Buddha-land, Amitābha Buddha's miraculous powers extend far beyond his land's inhabitants. He knows everything within infinite worlds, and every being's past actions, present actions, and karmic trajectory. Tathāgata Amitabha Buddha knows every single thought we have as ordinary beings, and a single drop of rain falling in our world. Therefore Amitābha Buddha definitely knows our repeat of His name. Amitābha Buddha also knows the vows we make; Amitābha Buddha also knows the moment our karmic retribution body is about to expire; Amitābha Buddha knows and foresees whether we were to die suddenly. From this, it is evident that we do not need to know the details of our final moments; when the time comes,

Amitābha Buddha will come because Amitābha Buddha already knows the exact moment of death. Amitābha Buddha will arrive at that moment of approaching death of his believers because that is his original vow, his testament with us. As long as we have ever repeated the Buddha's name with the intention of rebirth, even for a few seconds in our entire lifetime, or ten times of *Namo Amitābha*, we will still see Amitābha Buddha upon death. Moreover, according to the practice of the 5th grade, if we have practiced the Eight Precepts for a day and night and dedicated the merits for rebirth, our connection with rebirth has already been established. Thus, regardless of the various circumstances of our approaching death, we will be receivedby Amitābha Buddha and his retinue and be reborn.

This understanding is corroborated by descriptions of the scenarios where Amitabha Buddha manifests before the dying in the Nine Grades of Rebirth. One of the most evident instances is found in the 7th grade: "Those who are to be reborn in the Lower Grade high Birth may include sentient beings who commit numerous evil deeds... When their lives end... hearing the names of various scriptures, they have their extremely heavy evil karma accumulated for thousands of kalpas eradicated, and repeat of the Buddha's name will help eliminate their karmic consequences of fifty billion kalpas of birth and death. At that moment, the Buddha sends forth transformational body with his assembly Avalokiteśvara, Mahāsthāmaprāpta, and Mahāmaitreya before the dying person". The emphasis we want to highlight here is that at the moment of approaching death, Amitābha Buddha sends forth transformational body to appear before the person. The Buddha that one sees upon death is not a visualization conjured by the individual repeating the Buddha's name, but a radiance from the real Buddha in the form of his transformational body, which results from a behavior of the real Buddha in the Pure land. Furthermore, the evildoer does not inherently possess the ability to visualize the Buddha. Instead, it is Amitābha Buddha who, through his merit-reward-body in the Land of Ultimate Bliss, dispatches transformational emanations in the forms of Buddhas, Avalokiteśvara, and Mahāsthāmaprāpta to come to the individual's side. In other words, the appearance of Amitābha Buddha upon one's death is an act of Amitābha Buddha himself. It is entirely determined by Amitābha Buddha and not by the actions of the practitioner at the time, nor is it summoned or visualized by the practitioner's will during their dying moments. While the descriptions of Lower Grade sentient beings may carry some ambiguity regarding their approach to death and hearing the Dharma, the appearance of the Buddha at the moment of death is even more pronounced in the 3rd grade: "Those who are to be reborn in the high Class Lower Birth... when the practitioner's life is about to end, Amitābha Buddha, Avalokiteśvara, and Mahāsthāmaprāpta along with their retinues come holding golden lotus flowers and transform into five hundred Buddhas to receive the practitioner." When the practitioner's life is about to end, the emanations of Amitābha Buddha come to receive the person, offering solace and assurance to the practitioner. This occurrence is not determined by the practitioner's own will; it solely depends on whether the practitioner has receivedthe requirements of any grade within the Nine Grades. The differences among the Nine Grades primarily revolve around the specific scene of the appearance of the emanated Buddha and retinues at the moment of approaching death. Yet, it is apparent that the appearance of the emanated Buddha is dispatched by the merit-reward-body Buddha and is meant to receive the departing soul of the dying individual. Amitābha Buddha sends forth transformational emanations to receive the dying and prepare to escort them; they are not summoned by the dying individual. The whole apparition is not determined by conscious control of the dying person. In the natural occurrence of death, when and how death happens is not determined by us. The exact moment of our death is not determined by our will. Whether death occurs due to an earthquake, tsunami, nuclear explosion, sudden stray bullet, mysterious illness causing a coma, or the gradual fading of consciousness in a peaceful death, as long as one has receivedthe requirements of any grade within the Nine Grades for rebirth, or has repeated the Amitābha Sūtra for a day and night, one will unquestionably be receivedby Amitābha Buddha guiding them toward rebirth. Buddha's wisdom and compassion far surpass ours; we need only have faith. Hence, the approaching-death-moment is not an issue for Pure land practitioners. It has already been resolved by the vow-power of Amitābha Buddha. The question regarding the state of consciousness at the time of approaching death is also not a problem; it is naturally determined with certitude by the process of Amitābha Buddha's appearance and guidance in the stage of approaching death. When those who have vowed to be reborn in the Pure land repeat the Buddha's name, the Buddha is aware of it. From the moment we make the vow for rebirth and repeat the Buddha's name, Amitābha Buddha is already minded, and this person is recorded of his or her testament with the Buddha.

In summary, whether following the practice of the Contemplation Sūtra or the Amitābha Sūtra, Pure land practitioners need not worry about their moment of approaching death. Amitābha's original vow is that those who hear his name and wish to be reborn will attain rebirth in his Pure land with just ten recitations of his name. To hear His name only upon death is not a must. The reading to emphasize the moment of death as critical for rebirth does not exist in any of the three Pure land scriptures. If we stick to our traditional understanding, extreme apprehension about the state of consciousness upon death, and belief in direct link between this consciousness and reborn, then the easiest method to assure rebirth would be to immediately jump off a tall building to suicide oneself. During the falling, one could continuously repeat the name of the Buddha and repeat Buddha's name until one's brains are dashed out on the ground. One would be repeating the

Buddha's name right before death, and thus secure rebirth. Clearly, this is an extremely absurd behaviour. However, if we don't fully comprehend why this behaviour is absurd – that is, if we don't precisely understand that rebirth is not determined by the dying believer's state of consciousness, but rather by the covenant formed through the critical behaviors during our life time (such as practicing the Eight Precepts, repeating the Buddha's name or Mahāyāna texts, generating Bodhi determination, etc.) and Amitābha Buddha – this absurd notion will persist and remain difficult to eradicate.

Our understanding and advocacy of rebirth in the Pure land are now fully expounded. Fundamentally, we emphasize and apply the approach of liberation through encountering favorable conditions to comprehend the causal standards for rebirth, to understand and harmonize the various Pure land sects, and to address the anxiety that practitioners of Pure land Buddhism might have in their practice. Our understanding is based on the Nine Grades of the Contemplation Sūtra and Master Shandao's commentaries on it. While we have elaborated on our interpretation of key passaage from the Amitābha Sūtra with great effort, we still maintain that, from the perspective of ordinary people, the Contemplation Sūtra holds a higher position than the Amitābha Sūtra. Master Shandao states that the Amitābha Sūtra is suitable for those who possess the faculties of a śrāvaka, while the *Contemplation Sūtra* is appropriate for ordinary people. However, the ultimate principle is liberation by encounter, with the lowest standard being "hearing the name and wishing to be reborn," as exemplified by the 9th grade of rebirth in the Contemplation Sūtra.

# Embarking on the Path of Rebirth in the Mahayana: The Liberation by Encounter

In the preceding sections, we have discussed Master Shandao's interpretation of rebirth into the Nine Grades, emphasizing the concept of liberation through encountering favorable conditions. We have also explored how the key passages of the Amitābha Sūtra explain the idea of attached-thought on Amitābha Buddha and aspiring for rebirth in the Pure land. In practice, we have mentioned that by observing the Eight Precepts for a single day and night while continuously reciting the Buddha's name, one can at least attain the 5th grade of rebirth. This method of rebirth has a solid scriptural foundation. Rebirth is not an exceedingly difficult matter but rather something easily attainable. To seek rebirth, one can rely on any of the Nine Grades of practice according to the *Contemplation Sūtra*.

Even if one relies solely on reciting the Buddha's name, one has to spend one to seven days. This suggests that reciting the Buddha's name extensively is meant to elevate one's rebirth status. However, this perspective doesn't align with the scriptures, as rebirth in the superior class entails distinct practices. Merely reciting the Buddha's name extensively for the purpose of elevating one's rebirth status is a self-centered endeavor and falls into the category of the individual's own liberation. Even extensive recitation of the Buddha's name would still result in one's rebirth in the Middle Class, which is meant for people with Hinayana tendency. This view does not accord with the scriptures. Furthermore, grounded in the mentality of Hinayana beliefs, an extensive recitation of the Buddha's name to foresee one's departing time and attaining rebirth at the moment of natural cessation, remains a personal pursuit. Pursuing such an approach essentially abandons the boundless compassion and the Other-Power aspect of Amitābha Buddha, it would be reliance on self-power. This self-centered intention becomes even clearer when expressed among fellow practitioners. If one were to emphasize how extensively they recite the Buddha's name to achieve natural cessation, others among the Pure land practitioners might feel inferior, losing deep faith. They might think they lack the same level of recitation-meditation and therefore cannot attain rebirth. However, as we have already shown, there is no need to worry about the state of consciousness at the time of death. Prediction of departing time or the occurrence of natural cessation is not the prerequisite for rebirth attainment.

We have extensively discussed various thresholds for rebirth in the preceding chapters, particularly highlighting the 5th grade. We emphasize that one can rest assured that a day and night of observing the Eight Precepts and reciting the Buddha's name will lead to rebirth. In other words, we have entrusted our matters of life and death to Amitābha Buddha. After a day and night of practicing precepts and reciting the Buddha's name, we will attain rebirth. However, based on this, our religious life after this day and night has acquired new significance. When we recite the Buddha's name again, it is not for the sake of our own rebirth, as that has already been resolved. Instead, when reciting the Buddha's name outside of the day and night of precepts, it is primarily an act of benefiting sentient beings around us. It is intended to establish connections between beings who can hear the Buddha's name and the Pure land, planting the seeds for their future liberation in the Pure land. If there are no other beings around when reciting the Buddha's name, then we recite with a mindset of gratitude towards Amitābha Buddha, thanking him for the inevitable salvation when we receive our ends.

Recitation of the Buddha's name establishes ties with the sentient beings who hear it, by providing them with the remote and near causes for rebirth in the Pure land. A vivid story in the *Sūtra of Golden Light* illustrates the Benefits of recitation of Buddha name. In the story, Elder Changliushui witnessed a group of fierce animals devouring ten thousand fishes in a dried-up pond. Out of compassion, he drove away the wild beasts. To save the fishes, he sought help from a king whom he himself had once cured. Twenty elephants were then dispatched to fetch water from a river and pour into the dried-up pond. Ultimately, the ten thousand fishes were saved. During this process, Elder Changliushui noticed that wherever he walked along the shore, the fishes in the pond followed him joyfully. Assuming that the fishes were hungry, he returned home for fish food, and fed them. After feeding them, the scripture narrates: *"Now that I can provide these fish with food and satiety, in future lives, I will provide them with dhāraṇī sustenance. Furthermore, I contemplate: In the past, I heard of a monk in a quiet place who recited Mahāyāna sūtras and so on. In those sūtras, it is said that if sentient beings hear the name of the Bhagavān of Splendid Virtue when they are approaching the end of life, they will immediately be reborn in the Thirty-Three Heaven. Now I shall explain the profound Twelve Links to these ten thousand fish and also recite the name of the Bhagavān of Splendid Virtue. At that time, in the realm of Jambudvīpa, there are two types of people: those who deeply believe in the Mahāyāna and those who slander and do not give rise to faith and joy of them. At this moment, Elder Changliushui thought, 'I shall now enter the water to explain the profound and wonderful Dharma to these fish,' and with this thought, he entered the water and spoke as follows: 'Homage to the past Bhagavān of Splendid Virtue, endowed with proper and all-knowing knowledge, good conduct, understanding the world, unexcelled worthy, trainer of people, teacher of heavenly and human beings, Buddha Bhagavān. In the past, Bhagavān of Splendid Virtue made this vow: If sentient beings in the infinite spaces, upon death, hear my name and dedicate the merits from doing so to attain rebirth, then after their lives have ended, they will immediately take rebirth in the Thirty-Three Heaven.' Elder Changliushui himself turned into a fish in the water and explained this profound and wonderful Dharma to all fishes in the pond...'*

*At that time, Elder Changliushui and his two sons, having explained the Dharma, turned back into human beings and returned home. Later, his guests gathered, drank alcohol, and lay down. At that moment, the earth trembled, and all ten thousand fishes died simultaneously. After their death, they were reborn in the Heaven of the Thirty-Three."* This subsequent part of the story reveals that the fishes later all died in an earthquake. However, as a result of Elder Changliushui reciting the name of the Bhagavān of Splendid Virtue and explaining the Twelve Links to them, the ten thousand fishes were reborn as heavenly beings. The reliance that Elder Changliushui placed on the far-reaching sound of the Eastern Bhagavān of Splendid Virtue's name and his recitation of it for the fish's sake echoes the principle of our Western Pure land. What is to be noted about the story is that the fish did not die immediately after hearing the name but rather receivedtheir end in the earthquake afterwards, when Elder Changliushui returned home, gathered with guests, and became inebriated.

Nevertheless, the fishes still attained rebirth. This scriptural story affirms the immense merits of merely hearing the Buddha's name. It demonstrates that those who hear a Buddha name with vow power can achieve rebirth, and thus we assert that the individual must have substantial virtuous roots and accumulated merits from their past lives to encounter the Pure land teachings in this present life. One possible cause from a past life could be that a Pure land practitioner had recited the Amitābha Buddha's name near us when we were not yet in human form. Due to this connection established in a past life, we, as human beings in this life, can come into contact with the Pure land teachings. This story signifies that we can perform acts for others similar to what Elder Changliushui did for the fishes in this life. We can recite the Buddha's name for our pets at home, the animals doomed for slaughter at the market, or mention Amitābha's name in the presence of family members and friends. We do not persuade them to believe in the Pure land teachings, but merely to bathe them in the boundless merits of the Buddha name. These actions sow in them the seeds for rebirth in the Pure land and establish our conduct as that of Mahāyāna practitioners.

When we find ourselves alone and reciting the Buddha's name, the motivation behind this practice is one of gratitude towards Amitabha Buddha, thanking him for granting us the assured rebirth in the after-life. This reasoning also provides the foundation for the establishment of our school of Cundi. Practitioners of the Cundi school do not merely recite the Buddha's name as their daily practice; instead, they engage in the recitation of Cundi mantras and visualization of the Bodhisattva Cundi (which is one excellent form of Avalokiteshvara) to achieve worldly benefits. These benefits encompass a wide range of secular aspirations: wealth, success, children's education and harmonious loving relationships.

Such pursuits are commendable because the ultimate question of our liberation from birth and death has been entrusted to Amitabha Buddha. We seek and aspire for worldly achievements not just to benefit ourselves but to act as role models, therefore the realization of all worldly values becomes a bridge that connects more people with the Dharma. My recitation of the Buddha's name spreads to the ears of other sentient beings, transforming the world full of suffering into a crucible for sowing the seeds of Amitabha.

In other words, we can perceive the world as a pre-Pure land, a realm to be bathed in the light of Amitabha Buddha. It is like the soil of a Pure land that has yet to fully manifest, or rather, a Buddha-land that has not yet attained purity. Our actions—our efforts in worldly accomplishments and our recitation of the Buddha's name to help others transcend the worldly realm—all become the path of a Bodhisattva. This is the significance of our religious life after the practice for the rebirth based on the encounters with favorable conditions of 5th grade.

Of course, such Bodhisattva practices are not mandatory for rebirth. It is not difficult, though, to do it or even naturally achieve it after understanding the practice of encountering favorable conditions and engaging in Bodhisattva actions. If lay practitioners aim solely for their own rebirth and liberation, they can indeed attain rebirth by following the practice described in the 5th grade, spending one single day and night to maintain precepts and reciting the Buddha's name without further religious engagement afterwards. The compassion of Amitabha Buddha is infinite light, shining upon all sentient beings aspiring for the Pure land.

Finally, although this book repeatedly contemplates the meanings of scriptures and annotations, its motivation is not scholarly or academic. The writing is intended for fellow practitioners within the Buddhist community, rather than the academic sphere. Our objective is to elucidate the inherent meaning of encountering favorable conditions for liberation as found in the *Contemplation Sutra* and its Commentary by Master Shandao. While we are confident that the theoretical aspects presented here are accurate, we hold a stronger belief that any reader who has the karma to come across this book will also have the karma to attain liberation through encountering favorable conditions. Such a person is destined to be connected to Master Shandao and Master Gaoqi, and to have significant karmic ties with Amitabha Buddha's Pure land. After reading this book, the reader gets fully acquainted with the explicit way to assured rebirth in the Pure land. *Namo Amitabha.*

# Epilogue

After over two decades' (1997-2022) dedication to the propagation of the Cundi Dharma, I, upon reflection, still believe that my organization and promotion of Master Shandao's theory of liberation through encountering favorable conditions has been my greatest contribution to Buddhism in my lifetime.

In order to differentiate between the liberation through encountering favorable conditions and the Japanese Jōdo Shinshū, I attempt here a brief explanation.

In the context of rebirth, three levels of understanding arise concerning the roles of self-power.

First, whether one can attain rebirth relies entirely on self-power cultivated through one's own practice.

This perspective attributes rebirth to one's present life's practice and the accumulation of personal merit, and one's evaluation of their own practice determines their confidence in attaining rebirth.

Second, the acquisition of other-power is based on the self-benefiting practices of this life. The amount of self-power is equivalent to the amount of other-power. This is a thesis in the middle.

Third, the source of rebirth's merit power is entirely the power and merit of Amitabha Buddha. This is complete reliance on other-power.

The third is further divided into two distinct subcategories. The first is the "Choice of the Practice of repeating the Buddha's Name," where one chooses whether they are virtuous or non-virtuous, and decides whether they can attain rebirth with ten recitations or by methodically focusing on the practice of "single-mindedness."

The other application of the concept of other-power is what we have summarized as the "Liberation through Encountering Favorable Conditions." In this context, no choosing is involved; encountering Pure land teachings and the guidance of a good spiritual adviser are also manifestations of other-power, arising from accumulated merits and karmic conditions from past lives.

In reality, even the perspective of "choosing the practice of repeating the Buddha's name" implies a form of self-power. When compared to the Liberation through Encountering Favorable Conditions, the idea of other-power is not fully realized. It still holds that individuals have the capacity to make choices and opt for the best methods and the most suitable practices.

Due to my limited access to Japanese Pure land Buddhism, a lack of extensive firsthand fieldwork, and the fact that Chinese Buddhist textual sources exclude Jōdo Shinshū, this paper can only speculate that Japanese Pure land Buddhism adopted Master Shandao's idea of Pure land as the theoretical basis. But it may, because of it, possess a singular adherence to Master Shandao, leading to an extreme rejection of other sects for theoretical reasons. Jōdo Shinshū fully embraces the role of other-power, with the price of excluding, even slandering all other Buddhist schools, rather than harmonious coexistence.

On the other hand, the Liberation through Encountering Favorable Conditions, despite being a more complete form of other-power, is characterized by comprehensiveness. It acknowledges the variations in karmic conditions and merits from past lives among people.

From the perspective of dependent origination, Liberation through Encountering Favorable Conditions is absolute. What one perceives as personal choices are actually manifestations of the joy and delights accrued from past-life practices. Once we consider these joys as criteria for the only universal truth, comparisons, differences, and judgments towards others arise, this inevitably leads to conflicts and attacks within sects during their development.

In light of this contrast, Liberation through Encountering Favorable Conditions may appear to carry a sense of predestined fate. However, this is the destiny of Amitabha Buddha, not our individual destinies. We are already seamlessly integrated with Amitabha Buddha, which is akin to how Shakyamuni Buddha was prophesized to become a Buddha from birth. Our encounter with Amitabha Buddha signifies the end of our life in the six-realm cycle.

We anticipate that the theory of Liberation through Encountering Favorable Conditions, as refined by Master Shandao, can enhance the faith of practitioners in attaining rebirth in the Pure land, thereby fostering the peaceful development of various Buddhist schools internationally. May the world be at peace. May the pure Dharma carry on.

Gao Qi Shi.

www.ingramcontent.com/pod-product-compliance
Lightning Source LLC
Chambersburg PA
CBHW071323120626
46546CB00002B/414

* 9 7 8 1 9 5 7 1 4 4 9 5 5 *